WATER GARDENS
IN A WEEKEND®

WATER GARDENS IN A WEEKEND®

Peter Robinson

hamlyn

First published in Great Britain in 2001
by Hamlyn, an imprint of
Octopus Publishing Group Ltd
2–4 Heron Quays, London E14 4JP

This edition published in 2005

Distributed in the United States and Canada by
Sterling Publishing Co., Inc.
387 Park Avenue South, New York, NY 10016

'In a Weekend' is the registered property of Sterling
Publishing Co., Inc., 387 Park Avenue South, New York, NY
10016, and is used by permission.

ISBN–13: 978-0-600614-75-3
ISBN–10: 0-600-61475-1

A CIP catalogue record for this book is available from the
British Library

Printed and bound in China

10 9 8 7 6 5 4 3 2 1

Note: The time allocation for all the projects in this book
does not include organizing the supply of electricity to
those water features that require a pump. This can take
time, especially if the feature is some distance from the
house or the nearest supply point.

CONTENTS

INTRODUCTION

Ample space and time were once essential aspects of having a water garden. Space was considered necessary because the perception of a water garden was as a large affair, in scale with other equally impressive features. Time was essential, because construction techniques and materials meant that days, if not weeks, had to be spent in digging and transportation.

As our houses and gardens have become smaller there have been significant advances in the materials and equipment available for making and maintaining water gardens, reducing the need for large amounts of space to contour deep and spacious areas of water surface.

Below The simplicity of this Japanese water feature epitomizes the contribution that small water features can make in the modern garden.

Despite the improvements in construction materials, however, there has been an understandable reluctance to introduce water into gardens through concerns about safety, a nervousness about introducing an element that has such variability and, most of all perhaps, the demands that will be made on limited leisure time in constructing and maintaining the water feature.

Over the last few years a distinct change has occurred in water gardening, and much of this anxiety has been dispelled. Water has become an altogether more subtle ingredient in the overall garden, and the water garden no longer consists of large areas of open water but is more likely to take the form of one or even more smaller features, frequently exploiting movement and sound to bring surprise and interest to small nooks and corners rather than dominating the design. They have also become more accessible to amateur gardens in placing fewer demands on time needed for building and maintenance. There are now water features that can be installed in minutes as long as there is a nearby electric socket and a suitable wall to fix them to.

What are water features?

The term 'water features' has come to be used to refer to installations that are generally quite small, that require little skill or expense in construction and that often include a small circulating pump to introduce movement. These features have added to the repertoire of the gardener but have not replaced the water garden. They have made it possible to introduce some of the charms of water that would not previously have been considered in smaller gardens, and to help the gardener gain confidence in using this versatile element to add more individuality to the garden.

Water features in history

Smaller water gardens and water features have allowed the modern gardener to complete the historical circle of water's use in garden design. The gardens of early China made use of 'rooms', where gardens were split up into smaller areas, with water an ingredient in at least one of them. Mounds of rock were often placed next to small pools to recreate images of lakes and mountains, and these arrangements were given added significance by the positioning of 'windows' in partitions or screens between the garden areas so that the feature could be viewed from other parts of the garden. Water had even greater significance in the Japanese garden, where it was represented in raked gravel around rocks if it was not possible to include water itself. Many smaller water features from Japanese gardens, such as the *tsukubai* and *shishi odoshi*, are now included in Western gardens.

In contrast to the symbolic and spiritual properties of water in oriental gardens, the role of water in gardens from the Mediterrantean countries and the Middle East was more concerned with refreshment, movement and exuberance. Canals and fountains brought life and relief to the heat and dryness of the climate, and their plans became increasingly sophisticated as engineering and construction skills developed with time.

The landscape movement of more recent garden history used water on an imposing scale, as man-made lakes and ornamental bridges made their

Left A stone wall, cobbles and sheet of clear water create a fascinating composition, even without the assistance of plants.

mark on large country estates in Britain. With vistas of natural water in the distance, the immediate environs of the house became formal, with parterres and raised pools, which often had larger ornate fountains in the centre.

Since then, the most significant contribution to garden style has been in the 'natural' movement, as greater informality has crept into small gardens, with water playing an important role, as it did in all the other garden styles. The modern garden, although small, enjoys a freedom in design, and water can play a variety of roles. Water gardens are moving away from rectangular, formal pools or kidney-shaped, informal ponds edged by a ribbon of crazy paving to more innovative

Above A perfectly crafted pool with an elegant, simple edging frames plants from the main viewpoint.

Right The water gushes through this pipe with just enough turbulence to excite the senses.

features that exploit stillness and reflections or the exuberance of a lively fountain. They need no longer be forbidding or time consuming, and as the following pages will show, they can be introduced to the garden without having to devote weeks of precious leisure time to their construction.

Streams

It is even perfectly possible to construct an artificial stream within two weekends. If it is to look comfortable in the garden, your stream will need to have a natural-looking beginning and end, and although a pool is often the most desirable and natural end to a stream, a hidden reservoir is an effective alternative to ensure that there is enough water. A source for a rocky stream is often a small raised pool that retains a small amount of water when the pump is turned off.

There are numerous variations on this theme, and in a small flat garden surrounded by walls or fences, one or both ends of the stream can be made to look as if emerging from or disappearing into a neighbouring garden. Such an illusion can be fostered by such devices as building a false, protruding, arch-like structure at the stream's point of entry at the bottom of the wall with the delivery pipe hidden inside the arch.

Cascading streams can be made if there is a mound of soil or an existing slope, whereas in a relatively flat garden streams can be designed and built in a slower, more meandering style.

Practicalities

None of the projects in this book needs advanced building skills to complete, and many require no more than the effort required to excavate a hole large enough to accommodate a reservoir that will contain sufficient water to produce a gently bubbling fountain. There are also suggestions on how to use many of the simple kits that are available for self-contained water features and ways in which features made in this way can be fitted into an existing garden.

Where mortar is needed, as in some of the stream features, the projects assume that you will use ready-mix. There are also hints on fixing rocks and pre-formed units securely.

When you have completed your water feature and it has become an established part of your garden, you may find that you want to extend it and add to it, and there are a number of suggestions for ways in which you can enhance your feature by adding a bridge or stepping stones or a decked area. As you gain experience and confidence, you may even find that introducing a small cobble fountain or a half-barrel with one or two fish is just the first step in creating an entire water garden.

Above Water, particularly in such features as this escapist fountain, can be exploited to the full in the eclectic nature of modern garden design.

When you think of introducing water into the garden, the first step is to decide four main points: what style of water feature you would like, what size it should be, where to site it and how much you want to spend.

PLANNING

STYLES OF WATER FEATURE

There is a water feature that will suit every type of garden, formal or informal, large or small, high or low maintenance. Even if the feature you eventually choose is one of those that can be constructed in a single weekend, spend time at the planning stage to make sure that you select a pool that matches your needs, your lifestyle and your budget.

An important consideration is whether the pool will be raised, partially raised or built so that the surface of the water is at ground level. Raised pools have many advantages, not the least being that their construction requires no digging out, while partially raised pools need less digging out than a wholly sunken pool. Raised pools are also excellent at reflecting light from the sky, which can alleviate the claustro-phobic effect of high fences in a small, narrow garden. They allow easier appreciation of the detail and scent of aquatic flowers, particularly if the sight or hearing of visitors to the garden is impaired. If the side walls of the raised pool are strong enough, they make excellent casual seats, and such a pool makes it easier for wheelchair-bound gardeners to enjoy and tend to the pool and plants.

Water features without plants

Despite their relative ease in siting compared to a large, still pool that contains marginal plants and water-lilies, small moving water features will nevertheless benefit if time spent is in the initial planning. In small gardens, where space is at a premium, take advantage of every nook and cranny, note the areas of shade, the height of boundary walls and viewing lines from windows.

The setting chosen for a small water feature will have a major influence on its success and will be a clue to the most suitable style of feature. Such a feature may lack size, but it will have a huge impact on the garden. Sometimes the most unexpected position will be the most successful, and you might find it useful to go around the garden with a few cobbles or a pot and place them in a variety of positions, going back each time to the main viewing point or sitting area to assess the suitability of each site. Often one particular position will stand out as the right place and will make an association with steps, plants or a wall that were originally overlooked but, when the water feature is installed, become a favourite vista in the garden.

Water features with plants

As soon as you decide to include plants and fish in a water feature, the planning must take their needs into account in addition to your own preferences. This usually means that the area allocated for a water garden increases to accommodate an adequate variety of plants. Small water gardens, such as half-barrels and stone troughs, are perfectly satisfactory as long as the severe limitations of their

Right A brimming urn can form the starting point in creating a Mediterranean style in a small garden.

Opposite In a small courtyard a raised pool can be used in the same way as a mirror to make a space seem bigger.

Right In an area of heavy shade, like this tiny niche, a recirculating feature like this drilled rock fountain can make a lively focal point.

Far right Small pools with tropical waterlilies require maximum sunshine.

Below This fountain has been positioned to get a striking contrast between the dark, shady background and the sparkling water.

Opposite Creating a sub-tropical atmosphere is very easy with water plants and the appropriate evergreens nearby.

size are taken into account in the choice and quantity of plants and fish. The plantsperson or gardener who is interested in attracting the greatest variety of wildlife into the garden will prefer to devote a larger proportion of the space to the water feature.

Size has an obvious bearing on what can be achieved in one or two weekends, but the garden pool that is large enough to have a good visual impact and ample space for a modest collection of plants and fish will require a surface area of at least 4.5–5 sq m (50–55 sq ft), which is achievable within two weekends.

The importance of creating a pool of an adequate size is not only related to the variety and numbers of plants and fish that may be accommodated, but also, more importantly, to the pool's ability to become a self-sustaining environment that is clear and healthy. In the context of this book, small is beautiful and, so long as the excavation can be completed in the first weekend of our time limits on construction, the larger it is the better.

Increasing the surface area by excavating only a shallow basin would,

however, be a recipe for disaster. Small garden pools require a minimum depth of 45cm (18in); they are better still if 60cm (24in) can be reached. This additional depth will provide a zone of water near the bottom that is reasonably constant in temperature and is filtered from the immediate glare of sunshine. For a pool to be healthy and clear, the conditions that cause green algae to flourish should be avoided:

these are shallow water in full sunshine. Green algae require two main conditions for rapid growth: strong light and adequate foodstuffs in the form of mineral salts that are dissolved in the water. The aim in the design of a garden pool, therefore, is to provide an environment that will deny them the mineral salts and shade out the summer light.

Conveniently, this is achieved in a well-balanced pool by other plants, the submerged plants (known as oxygenators), which use up the mineral salts, and the surface-leaved plants, like waterlilies, which shade out light. The large group of plants known as marginals play a part in both roles but are mainly used as decorative plants in the shallower fringes of the pool. In order to provide a suitable depth of water for the marginal plants the profile of the hole should include a shelf, which should be no more than 23cm (9in) deep and wide. Submerged plants and waterlilies grow from the bottom of the deeper zone, which remains free of frost in temperate winters.

Matching the surroundings

A good start in planning is to consider the age of the garden and property. A new house with nothing more than

builder's rubble or a freshly laid lawn becomes a clean canvas to develop any style you wish and the water feature could be the starting point for creating a style around it. In a small garden a large, brimming urn could suggest a Mediterranean-style garden, with clumps of graceful ornamental grasses and sweeps of gravel making for a perfect partnership.

If the garden has already been successfully developed and requires little change, deciding where to incorporate a feature in keeping with the existing style will be the challenge. The style and colour of the urn that were appropriate for the new garden may not fit in as well with older building materials, and here the surfaces could suggest an old stone trough, which would blend with the mellow stone and muted shades. It is unlikely there will be room for a large feature, so the planting and hard landscape materials around it will be particularly important in melding the water feature to the garden's age and style.

If the garden is in heavy permanent shade, a condition that would make it unsuitable for an open pool filled with waterlilies and, indeed, for most other aquatics, the low light levels could be used to advantage by creating a small, open raised or sunken pool that is surrounded by ferns.

Additional interest could be introduced by the addition of a quiet trickle of recirculating water or even a well-positioned light. This type of water feature works well when it is partly or totally hidden from the rest of the garden, and adding an element of surprise to a corner requires no more than the planting of a few carefully sited evergreen shrubs to provide an appropriate corner.

The main pleasure that a water feature will provide will lie in expressing your individuality, style and creativity. You may choose to create a fountain, so that you are invigorated by the sounds of splashing water, or you may

prefer to be refreshed as you relax by the calmness of a small reflective pool.

The shape of the pool will be governed by how best it will fit in to the surrounding garden. Regular shapes, such as circles, rectangles and squares, will fit into a formal garden where there are straight lines, neatly clipped hedges, plants in rows and steps and retaining walls on a sloping site. Formal pools fit well into paving surrounds, and if they have straight sides they are easier to incorporate near the house. Irregularly shaped pools fit best into informal gardens, where there are curving edges, shrub borders, plants in groups and sloping lawns if there is a gradient. The informal pool often fits well into the lawn.

Above right Bricks are ideal material for edging the tightly curving outline of small formal pools.

Right Formal pools set into a gravel surround will need an adequate margin of paving to emphasize the shape.

Left Edges of informal streams or pools are much better if softened with dense planting.

Sounds from water

Moving water features can produce an incredible variety of sounds, which are highlighted and reflected in small spaces bounded by high walls or fences. Place a simple, self-contained wall fountain in a conservatory and you will quickly realize how dominating it can be as the sound is reflected from above as well as from the sides.

When planning a feature with moving water, anticipate the impact of sound. If it is to be next to a sitting area, a sound suited to a bigger garden could be irritating to guests, particularly if it competes with conversation.

Make provision in the design for the noise level to be muted to a gentle trickle if the spout is near a social area. The ability to influence the level and type of sound is one of the reasons moving water features are so fascinating, and the slightest adjustment to the rate of flow can have enormous impact on the effects produced, particularly when water falls on to another water surface. The rate of flow, the height of the fall and how the water makes contact with the surface below, whether in drips, rivulets or weirs, have an effect on the sound. Small cascades are always popular, and if the water at the base of the cascade is deeper than 25cm (10in) falling water will make a quite different sound to water falling onto cobbles or a shallow pool, where splash becomes a part of the effect. Generally, the effect of water sound will be more exhilarating as the volume of moving water increases. In contrast, a gentler, less turbulent flow will produce a more peaceful, calming result.

SITING

Identifying the best site for a pool that will support plant life is often a process of elimination, and it can be a useful exercise to draw a simple plan on which you identify the main features. Maximum sunshine is important for warming the water in spring and vital to flowering of waterlilies. Finding which parts of the garden receive sunshine for most of the day should be marked on your scale plan first.

Next, identify the shady parts, noting, first, the areas in permanent shade, and second, the areas that are in shade for only part of the day. The shaded zones indicated on the plan should also indicate dappled shade, such as the light shade cast from small lightly branched trees, and the heavy shade from tall buildings or heavily branched, large trees. The direction of prevailing winds should be noted, too, especially where there are deciduous trees in the garden. The leaves of some trees, such as walnut, can be toxic if they are allowed to accumulate in a small pool, and you may have to consider netting the surface or the perimeter of the pool if autumn leaves are likely to be blown into the water.

Avoiding hazards

Features in the garden that should be avoided, such as established specimen plants, sheds, greenhouses and steps, should be marked on the plan, as

Right In a large expanse of gravel, ivy has been used to good effect to contrast with and give emphasis to the hard circular edge of the pool.

WHERE TO SITE YOUR POND

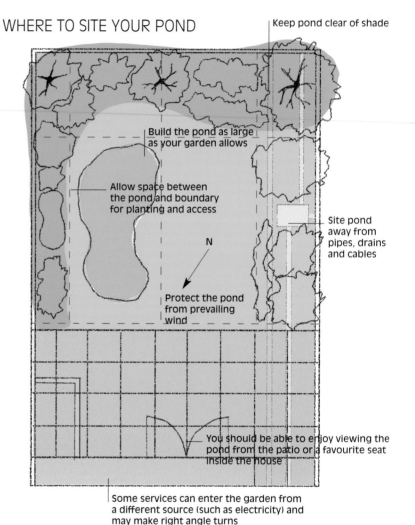

Keep pond clear of shade

Build the pond as large as your garden allows

Allow space between the pond and boundary for planting and access

N

Protect the pond from prevailing wind

Site pond away from pipes, drains and cables

You should be able to enjoy viewing the pond from the patio or a favourite seat inside the house

Some services can enter the garden from a different source (such as electricity) and may make right angle turns

should the underground services like gas, water, electricity, telephone and drains. If there are no plans showing the routes of these services and they are not obvious from the position of manholes, contact service providers, who have portable detectors to help identify their location.

Finally, mark the viewlines from frequently used windows and from the patio if you have one.

Positioning the pool

Cut a piece of cardboard roughly to the shape of the proposed pool and in scale to the size of your plan, and move it around on the plan until you find a suitable position. This may have to be a compromise. Transfer this position to the actual garden and as a final check mark the outline with canes, a hosepipe or sand so that it can be viewed from the house windows.

Planning

SAFETY

The introduction of a water feature into a garden has implications for safety, not only from the presence of expanse of open water but also because electricity is needed to power submersible pumps. It is not just wildlife that is attracted to water: toddlers find it irresistible and every precaution should be taken to place water out of bounds when children are unsupervised.

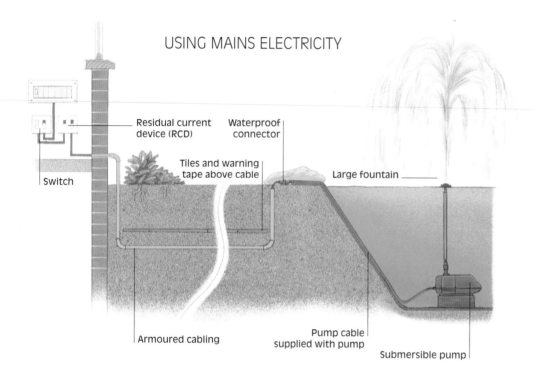

USING MAINS ELECTRICITY

Switch

Residual current device (RCD)

Waterproof connector

Tiles and warning tape above cable

Large fountain

Armoured cabling

Pump cable supplied with pump

Submersible pump

USING LOW-VOLTAGE ELECTRICITY

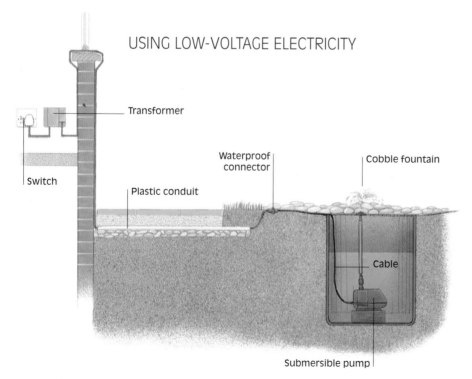

Transformer

Switch

Plastic conduit

Waterproof connector

Cobble fountain

Cable

Submersible pump

Electricity in the garden

The introduction of electrical appliances, such as pumps and submerged lights, into water can also be a cause for concern. Although modern appliances are insulated and safe to use in water, they should be used with a circuit breaker, a small device connected to the cable from the pump or lighting between it and the mains supply socket. These cut off the current within 30 milliseconds if the supply is accidentally earthed.

Electrical equipment is supplied with integral waterproof leads. Most pumps, for example, have leads 10m (30ft) long, and this is usually more than enough to extend well beyond the sides of a garden pool. The lead should be joined to an approved waterproof socket, which can be hidden near the pool. Alternatively, the lead can be connected to a waterproof outdoor switchbox, and these are

---

Practicalities

Pump problems

The most likely problems in small fountain features will be mechanical or structural, and probably be related to a failure in the electricity supply or a malfunction in the pump. The most common fault in the cobble-type fountain feature results from the reservoir running dry while the pump continues to work. The pump overheats and fails. In hot, dry weather regularly check the level of water in reservoir.

available with two or three outlet connections. Slightly more expensive are three-way switches, which make the connection of extra equipment at a later date much easier.

The cable supplying the switchbox from the supply should be special cabling for outdoor use. It is known as armoured cabling and has a protective sheath that is strong enough to withstand accidental damage from a spade or fork while you are gardening. As an extra precaution, lay the cable in a trench 30–60cm (1–2ft) deep and place bricks or roofing tiles over it. Lay plastic warning tape over this.

For small water features and pools, low-voltage pumps and lights may be adequate, and this equipment does not require the protection of a contact circuit breaker or armoured cabling. Protection is provided by reducing the current through a transformer designed for internal or external use. The improved efficiency of low-voltage halogen bulbs makes low-voltage applications ideal for garden lighting, but check that the pump is adequate for fountains like geyser jets or for circulating a large volume of water through a tall urn or waterfall.

It cannot be stressed too often that water and electricity are a lethal combination. Always use waterproof armoured cable and a waterproof connector and always employ a qualified electrician to advise on the layout of the system and install the fittings for water features.

Children and water

Parents are naturally anxious about the safety of very young children when there is any exposed water in the garden. One of the simplest methods to reduce the danger is to cover the pool with a panel of galvanized steel mesh. This is obtainable at builder's merchants in panels measuring 2 x 1m (6 x 3ft), and it is mainly used as reinforcement for concrete drives and pathways. Thick plastic mesh can also be

Above This safety grid on the water surface is built not only to be functional but to add ornament to the pool.

INSTALLING A PROTECTIVE GRID

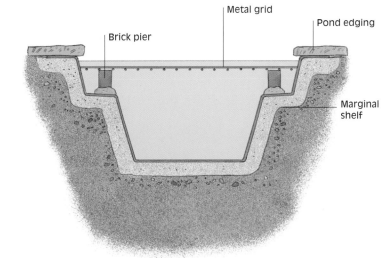

Brick pier
Metal grid
Pond edging
Marginal shelf

used provided it is stapled onto a strong wooden grid approximately 30cm (12in) square. The mesh can be laid on top of the pool and secured by heavy stones but a much more attractive method is to support the mesh just under the water surface on brick piers built temporarily on the marginal shelves just inside the pool edges. The mesh is almost completely obscured,

and any plants with upright leaves will grow through the squares and have added support against wind. Once the the danger to children is over, the cover can be removed one winter when vegetation has died down and is no longer entangled in the mesh.

Remember that materials used to edge pools should be non-slip (see page 107).

The range of material available for constructing water features has grown considerably in recent years, allowing you to introduce quite complex water features with the minimum of building work and disruption to the rest of the garden.

MATERIALS

FLEXIBLE LINERS

For versatility in use and economy in cost, flexible liners are the ideal choice for waterproofing open pools and sunken reservoirs. The liners are available in an almost unlimited range of sizes and can be obtained from local garden and aquatic centres and by mail order. In garden centres liners are sold from rolls, and for most small pools the roll width will be adequate.

Practicalities

Choosing a Liner
Take the following factors into account when you are making your choice:

- **Stony ground or made-up ground containing sharp edges**. Careful preparation can do much to avoid the risk of the liner being pierced, but in a very stony plot it would be sensible to choose one of the thicker materials together with a good underlay.

- **The depth of the pool or reservoir**. The greater the depth, the greater the pressure that is placed on the liner at the pool bottom. All the liners available will be able to resist this pressure in the pools described in this book, but on stony ground, where there is a greater risk of an unnoticed hazard, select a stronger material.

- **Exposure to prolonged sunlight**. In open pools there is often a thin strip of liner above the water level that is totally exposed to sunshine. Some of the cheaper liners are vulnerable in this respect, and the liner will harden and crack with time, so if the proposed site is very sunny, make sure that the liner is resistant to deterioration in ultraviolet light.

- **Colour**. Some types of liner are available in different colours, but there is no need to consider anything but black because algae will eventually cover the submerged surface and the dark colour gives a greater illusion of depth.

- **Irregular or serpentine outlines**. One of the problems with all flexible liners is in forming folds in corners or curving outlines. When these are excessive, a liner that has a greater degree of elasticity allows the folds to be less conspicuous because the liner is stretched into the mould.

Top and above A strong underlay is laid over the whole excavation, with extra on vulnerable spots. Then the flexible liner is draped into the hole and held in place with bricks until the pool is filled.

Mail order specialists tend to have a greater range of sizes and types, and can arrange for 24- or 48-hour delivery.

After working out the size, choose the sort and thickness of flexible liner from the 3–4 main types. As the manufacture of each type has improved, the wide variations between the different types have diminished, and for a small pool of the kind that can be built in two to three weekends, there should be no problem in using any of them as long as you take a few precautions. A reasonable guide to quality will be the guarantee that is available with each type, and, as with most things, the rule of thumb is that the more you pay, the better the guarantee.

Polythene (polyethylene)
The first liner to be used for pools in the late 1930s, polythene is now mainly used in the building industry. It is sold in large sheets for lining industrial projects, where its susceptibility to ultraviolet light – it hardens and cracks – is not important. In ornamental pools, however, this was its downfall, because pools made of it soon cracked and leaked. It is also somewhat unwieldy

and stiff. It should be considered only for lining reservoirs under moving water features where there is no exposure to light and cheapness is a factor.

Low-density polythene (LDPE)

This is such an improved form as to be unrecognizable from the stiff sheets of polythene described above. This is sold widely under various tradenames and has the same benefit of cheapness but is nowhere near as stiff and difficult to handle. Various grades are available, with a range of time limits on the guarantees. It is superb for lining the reservoirs under water features, but choose the better quality grades that specify ultraviolet resistance if it is to be used in sun. Standard polythene cannot be repaired, but thicker grades of this improved material can be patched with double-sided repair tape.

PVC

A middle-of-the-range liner, PVC has been widely used over the years and is still popular. It superseded polythene in the 1950s and 1960s, when small pools were increasing in popularity. PVC has a good life-expectancy – 10 to 20 years – and is available in different thicknesses. Some grades have been reinforced with a nylon mesh sandwiched as a middle layer for extra strength. Pieces of it can be welded together, and repair kits are available.

Butyl and rubber liners

The appearance of butyl in gardening coincided with a new wave of popularity in ornamental pools. The material had previously been used in building as a roofing material, but its elasticity in comparison with other materials soon made it apparent that it was a very suitable product for lining pools.

This and closely related products continue to be used by professional installers of large water gardens, for their elasticity and durability. They can be used in full sunlight and where there are likely to be several folds in a

Left Flexible liners allow great freedom in design and are ideal for informal pools surrounded by dense planting.

mould. They are probably the most expensive liners, but are undoubtedly the best and would appear to have an indefinite life expectancy.

Underlays

Soft sand was once used as a protective lining under the waterproofing liner, but a range of geotextile membranes is now available on the domestic market which are more effective. The thinner forms are sold as frost protective 'fleece' coverings, but the thicker types are suitable for protection in pool excavations. Tempting though using old newspaper to cushion the liner may seem, it quickly rots in damp soil and leaves the liner unprotected. Old carpet is better, although it is rather unwieldy to use in small areas.

Practicalities

Repairing a liner

One of the worst nightmares of the pool owner is a leaking pond. Modern liners or pre-formed pools are unlikely to leak because the production methods in their manufacture are so good. Accidents can occur, however, and liners are pierced with gardening tools or the claws of large dogs. Herons, too, can pierce liners as they stab the shallow water with the sharp tips of their beaks. Flexible liner leaks are repaired by applying a waterproof, double-sided, adhesive tape, which is available from aquatic retailers or the liner suppliers. Clean the area around the damage with a soft cloth and dab it with an alcohol-based cleaner. Place the repair tape over the puncture and allow it to become tacky before you place a patch of spare liner onto the tacky surface, pressing it down firmly to flatten the edges. Allow at least a few hours to elapse before refilling the pool with water.

RIGID PRE-FORMED LINERS

The sight of the ready-made pools displayed in garden centres is a tempting one for the weekend gardener, for whom ease and speed of installation are the major considerations in choosing which type of pond to add to the garden. There are now so many shapes and thicknesses of material that there is probably one outline to suit nearly every small pool scheme.

Planting is made easier for the novice because marginal shelves are moulded into the outline, and suggested planting guides are even given with many types to indicate the number of different plant types that the particular shapes will need. The volume of each shape is also indicated, making the future application of chemicals like algaecides easier to calibrate.

As with flexible liners, a wide range of materials is used in their manufacture, but it is worth bearing in mind that the strongest types can be expensive when compared with a flexible liner for the same-sized pool. Remember, too, that although they look enormous on their sides in the showroom, when they are buried in the ground they seem to be only half the size. The extra expense is probably justified for very small pools, and the installation of these requires no more than marking out the outline on the site and digging a hole to correspond to the shape. In some cases there is no need to dig a hole to the full depth of the outline because they make excellent semi-raised pools, where only the deeper zone is buried. This is particularly suitable on sloping sites, where the lower side of the pool can be disguised with a rock garden or low wall.

The rigidity of the outline suits formal simple shapes, such as squares, rectangles and circles, when the edge is easier to disguise with paving. Avoid fussy shapes with long, narrow necks and serpentine edges. Their edges are much more difficult to disguise in an informal setting, and they can be more prone to algal

growth where the water tends to warm up too much in narrow bits.

It is tempting to skimp on the preparation of the hole with pre-formed pools, but you can only dare risk this with the expensive, thick fibreglass types, which are strong enough to have small parts of their frame suspended without cracking. When these pools are full of water they are incredibly heavy, and if not given adequate support they can bend easily, resulting in serious sinkage of the sides and, worse still, cracking of the frame.

1

Whereas there is little difference in the appearance of flexible liners, there is a huge difference in the colours and quality of finish of rigid units, and it is well worth spending some

2

3

time looking at the different types that are available at various retail outlets before making your choice.

Fibreglass

The strongest pre-formed pools are those that are made with fibreglass and finished with a polished surface on the inside of the pool, an advantage that makes it easy to clean off the algae. Most of the colours are sympathetic to gardens, but you should avoid any that are made in bright or light colours, which are difficult to disguise, especially along the area between the water surface and the rim of the pool.

Reinforced plastic

Thick reinforced plastic pools come a close second in strength and durability to fibreglass. They are generally black in colour. They do have some 'give' in them and bend easily along the rim if the pool lacks support from the soil outside the shell. They cost between one-half and two-thirds of the price of the fibreglass pools and are available in a very wide variety of shapes.

1 A high density rigid polyethylene pool 137cm (54in) across.

2 A formal rigid high density polyethylene pool 180 x 130cm (70 x 51in)

3 An informal shape in rigid high density polyethylene 203 x 124cm (80 x 49in)

4 A rigid rock stream unit in ultraviolet-resistant resin, 122 x 74cm (48 x 29in)

Vacuum-formed plastic

The cheapest units available are made in a thinner type of vacuum-formed plastic. Because of their relative thinness, the profiles can be moulded into more intricate designs than the more expensive, thicker units. They are restricted in overall size because of their lack of rigidity, but as pre-formed pools are only economic to buy for small pools when compared to flexible liners, this is unlikely to be a major issue.

Stream units and rock pools

Pre-formed pools come into their own in stream units and rock pools, which can be fitted easily into a slope next to a pool to provide a recirculating stream. This type of construction brings a small stream within the scope of a completely unskilled person and can be completed in a very short time.

The most natural-looking stream will be created when rocks and flexible liners are used, as these materials offer scope for enormous creativity, but rocks can be heavy and incorporating liners with rocks into waterfalls is definitely a more skilled operation, often involving the use of mortar. Rigid stream units, on the other hand, incorporate a lip to pour the flowing water into a similar unit below, making their installation a simple matter. When they are designed with subtle changes of direction and the edges are hidden by scrambling plants, they can be made to look very acceptable in a small informal watercourse.

Some stream units have small pockets or depressions, allowing shallow water to remain in the stream when the pump is off, and these mini-pools form superb bird baths.

Pre-formed rock pools are wider and deeper than the stream units, and they are intended to be used either as header pools to form the source of the stream or as small pools incorporated into the stream sections. They can be

4

used to make separate rock pools quite independent of a stream provided they are adequately planted with an aquatic plant mixture to keep down the green algae.

It is worth researching the many different types of rigid stream unit that are available, not only to find a design that will suit your proposed scheme, but also to find a colour and texture that will blend in well with the surrounding areas in your garden. There is a very wide range to choose from, and some models are more realistic and effective than others.

Advances in constructing simulated rocks and cobbles are being made constantly, and each spring sees a rash of new designs. One of the most effective is a rigid fibreglass unit with a sandblasted finish, giving a very realistic sandstone rock effect. The more common units are made in a grey 'limestone' texture, and they are available in different lengths with matching intermediate rock pools to give variety and a more natural look.

Below The edges of this preformed pool are beautifully disguised by bricks.

Materials

TRADITIONAL BUILDING MATERIALS

Bricks and mortar still have their place in constructing small water gardens, but they do require basic building skills in tasks like laying walling blocks, bricks and concrete. Pools made from concrete are now mainly the domain of specialist fish-keepers, who require deep pools with vertical side walls, preferably above ground level.

Such pools are not within the scope of this book. The substantial investment necessary for keeping collections of koi as a serious hobby involves considerable pipework, filters and drains to maintain immaculately clean water without plants so that specimen fish of enormous value can be safely housed.

There are, however, occasions when building materials are recommended in this book for use in some of the larger projects, such as the making of simple, strong supports underneath water features like brimming urns or in laying hard surfacing materials around a water feature in a formal situation.

Using mortar

The two more ambitious projects, which take three weekends – making a simple canal and a rocky stream with waterfalls – require mortar during the construction process. Even here,

though, it is not a major part of the construction process and does not require any high levels of building skills. The mortar is obtainable in ready-mixed bags, and the only specialist tools that you will need will be a small pointing trowel, instead of the rather rounder and thicker gardener's trowel, and a spirit level.

Mention is made in some of these projects of special reinforcing fibres, which are added to the mortar mix (see pages 102–103). These are small, white fibre strands, which are added to the ready-mix at the same time as the water. They are extremely useful when mortar is needed in projects in water gardening, because they help to prevent any movement of the mortar that may cause hair-line cracks and the consequent possibility of slow leaks.

Bricks and terracotta

Wherever decorative bricks are to be used in contact with water, use engineering bricks if possible as they are water resistant. They are dark in colour and may not be suitable in those situations where a more traditional brick colour is required. Speak to your supplier when buying bricks and explain that you need hard bricks that will be less vulnerable to frost damage when wet. If the softer, more absorbent bricks are the only type available, paint them with a proprietary water sealant. You should also use this sealant to paint any terracotta products that you plan to use as tipping or brimming urns. Terracotta is more vulnerable to frost when it is wet, and the containers should be given two or three coats of sealant, inside and out, before use.

Right Where bricks are in contact with water, ensure that they are waterproof or sealed with a waterproofing sealant when completely dry.

Left Although costly, reclaimed granite setts can be used to great effect as pool surrounds in cottage or period gardens.

Practicalities

Repairing hairline cracks in concrete ponds

Cracks are most likely to occur in old concrete ponds that have developed fine hairline cracks over the years through slight movement of the surrounding soil or weaknesses in the original mix. Repairing the crack involves draining the pool to just below the suspect point so that the surface can be dried out. The point of the leak can often be identified by the pool remaining at a constant level just below the leak. When you have found the leak, clean the surrounding area with a wire brush. Chisel out a shallow groove along the crack and fill the groove with mortar using a pointed trowel. Smooth it over and leave to dry for a day or two. When the mortar is completely dry, apply a coat of a proprietary pool-sealing compound, which also prevents the lime in the mortar from dissolving into the water. Ensure that the sealant is colourless as a black or white paint could be conspicuous in the clear water.

CONTAINERS

A pool in miniature is one of the easiest of water gardens to construct, and some of the simplest water features are based on containers that you may already have in the garden or that are widely available from garden centres and DIY stores. Not every container is suitable for this purpose, however, because the water in a very shallow container in full sun will be difficult to keep clear.

The water will heat up quickly on sunny days, so resist the temptation to keep fish, no matter how small they are, if the depth of the container is less than 38cm (15in), unless it is in permanent shade. Containers that are less than 15cm (6in) deep are not really suitable for planting because they might freeze solid in a severe cold spell unless they can be given temporary shelter in a greenhouse or conservatory. If very shallow containers, such as small bowls, are to be used, they should be placed in shade, and you will have to change the water when it goes green.

When you replace the water, try to use rainwater rather than tapwater, which contains both chlorine and the mineral salts that encourage the rapid growth of algae. A very small container placed in full sunlight could, however, be successful as part of a moving water system where the water can trickle in and out on its way to a larger reservoir of water.

Right If positioned in full sunlight, very small containers will need the water changing regularly or it will go cloudy.

Practicalities

Avoiding problems

If running continuously in dry, hot weather, fountains can lose a considerable volume of water through evaporation. There are two important details in the successful running of these features: first, make sure that the reservoir is large enough to cope with the considerable demands placed on it; and second, make sure that the vertical pipe from the pump is as high as possible inside the urn. If the end of the pipe is too low, all the water above the pipe returns through the pump into the reservoir when the pump is turned off. If the reservoir is too small there is a chance that it will overflow every time the pump stops, with the consequent loss of water in the reservoir.

Sinks and troughs

Stone sinks and troughs are becoming increasingly rare, and their cost has risen accordingly. Because of this, you may find it easier to simulate a natural stone trough by coating a suitable container with a material called hyper-tufa, which weathers into a stony appearance and has a rough surface that, with a little help, will allow the growth of algae. Although old glazed sinks are becoming almost as rare as stone sinks, these may be found in reclamation yards specializing in recycled building materials and are generally deeper than real stone troughs.

Half-barrels

Recycled barrels that have been cut in half are now fairly commonplace in garden centres for use as planters. They also make excellent small water features, where they can be used entirely above ground or partially sunk into the ground. You may be lucky enough to find one that will hold water without waterproofing, and if you are choosing a half-barrel that is displayed outdoors, look inside to see if it has held any rainwater. The more moisture that the timbers in the barrel have been subjected to, the more likely it is that they will have remained swollen and watertight. Look for barrels on which the supporting metal hoops are still intact, indicating that the staves have remained firmly in position. When the barrel is refilled the hoops will provide the necessary support against the water pressure. Avoid cheaper timber containers that have been made to simulate barrels.

Choose the largest size possible to allow as much creativity in the planting and the possibility of having two or three small goldfish, which will come to no harm in summer in the larger barrels if these are well planted and in partial shade.

Urns

Much of the pleasure in making the project described on pages 58–9 will be in choosing an urn that pleases the eye. However, it must also be an urn that can be lifted easily, which means one that is no more than 45cm (18in) high. One of the most important details to look for is a rim that is quite level. An urn that has a thick, uneven rim will not produce the even film of water over the sides necessary to achieve the best effect. Sandpapering the rim with very rough sandpaper to achieve a more even surface is well worth the time and effort. The evenness of the rim can be checked by standing the urn on a perfectly level surface and pouring water from a hose inside until it overflows. Keep the water flowing at a steady rate or it may be much more powerful than the pump and not a fair test.

Some urn shapes are more appropriate for the brimming effect than others. If the water is to cling to the urn sides, the body of the urn should be fatter than the rim, and the increase in width should start very near the top. Obviously, in a straight-sided or typical pot-shaped urn, where the sides gradually narrow to the bottom, the water will fall away from the sides.

When you are choosing an urn, check that it will be resistant to frost.

Left An old stone trough makes an excellent reservoir for a small wall fountain.

Left In order to achieve this even flow, this urn has to be set dead level.

Far left Waterlilies need full sunlight, so make sure that any taller plants in a barrel are not casting shadow on to them.

Many terracotta items, such as urns, are frost sensitive, particularly when damp or wet. If the urn is to be kept out of doors for the winter in climates prone to frost, it is vital that it will not crack. Frost resistance is greater in terracotta when the urn is dry. It is strongly recommended that the first thing to do when you get the urn home, while it is still completely dry, is

to paint the inside and out with two or three coats of a proprietary water sealant, allowing each coat to dry thoroughly before applying the next. This will prevent the terracotta absorbing moisture, which will make it more frost proof. The sealant has a double bonus, because the sealed surface is smoother and the water tends to flow over it more easily.

Materials

SELF-ASSEMBLY KITS

Kits designed for moving water features – cobble fountains, tipping urns and wall fountains, for example – have become more commonplace, and they are very relevant to the theme of this book. Most of these can be installed easily within a weekend, and it is likely that providing the electricity supply will be more time consuming than installing the feature.

Right Pebble fountain kits come in a variety of sizes and shapes, including circular, and are usually made in high density polyethylene.

Below A small circular kit above installed in three or four hours.

Mass-produced kits do not mean that identical features need to be seen on every patio. Individuality can be introduced by the setting and styling of the surroundings, and variations in planting and hard surfaces mean that no two features need look the same. As with pre-formed pools and stream units, it pays to shop around to find the widest available variety because new products and styles are being manufactured each year to meet the increasing demand for small water features.

Cobble fountains

Of the many fountains now available for quick installation into a garden, the cobble fountain must rank as the most popular. One of the great advantages of this type of fountain is the enormous number of variants that have evolved from the basic construction. These features are now widely available in kit form, and the wide range of surfacing materials and settings in which they look comfortable makes them justifiably among the most successful small moving water features.

The cobble fountain can be as large or small as you wish as long as the volume of the reservoir is adequate and the loss of water through evaporation in sunny, windy weather does not necessitate too-frequent topping up. There are several surfacing materials that can be used to cover and surround it to add individuality and an element of surprise. Too often the cobble fountain is set in a tight circle of cobbles, all the same size and colour and quite unrelated to the adjacent garden. Although it is illegal to collect cobbles from the beach in many countries, an increasing variety of cobbles, pebbles, ornamental gravels and small rocks is available at specialist landscape centres, and these are worth seeking out to add a personal, individual touch.

Wall fountains

In addition to the popular bubble fountains, with cobbles and millstones, it is also possible to buy self-contained wall fountain kits, which require no more than screwing to the wall and plugging into an adjacent socket. The kits contain a small reservoir, tiny submersible pump, a marked position for the supporting screws and an electric lead with the plug already fitted. They are made of resin, rigid PVC or cast iron, and most require no painting or maintenance. Many of the designs are based on traditional masks, such as the heads of lions or goddesses, with the small spout of water emerging from the mouth.

If the kit has an integral pump, the installation is straightforward. If it is sold without an integral pump, be very careful to check that there is adequate room in the reservoir for the pump and that the pipework can be satisfactorily sealed.

The cheaper kits have no provision for altering the rate of flow, so the sound cannot be varied. In a confined space, particularly a conservatory, this can be quite intrusive and may not have the desired soothing effect that falling water can have.

Before purchasing one of these kits, try to find a centre where one is operating and listen to it for a minute or two, trying to imagine this effect in your own garden. Also try to imagine how the mask and bowl will blend with the wall and surroundings. They are normally only about 60cm (2ft) tall and

45cm (18in) wide, and if placed alone on a vast expanse of bare wall, might look out of scale and rather lonely. If you use a mass-produced kit you need to pay particular attention to the surroundings, as these items generally look better if there is some surrounding planting or ornamental trellis on the wall, especially when you have to disguise the cable connecting the wall feature to an electric socket.

Several wall fountain manufacturers supply matching spill basins and masks, but many of these basins are extremely heavy and require strong fixings to the wall.

In some cases they require the construction of a false wall to give enough support to the basin's weight. These are beyond the scope of the weekend allowed for the construction of the feature, but there are some lighter and less sophisticated basins, which can be simply bracketed to the wall to catch the water spout then overflow into the pool. These are made in lightweight materials rather than reconstituted stone or concrete, and they are often in the form of a scallop shell, which is a popular shape for the basin as it channels the water into fine, thread-like strands.

Above A wall fountain installed onto a freshly made low false wall behind which the pipework is hidden. A lighter version would not need this extra support.

PUMPS

Create a moving water feature and, unless you are using a kit that comes supplied with all the appropriate items, you will need to buy a pump. When you visit an aquatic centre, choosing a suitable model from the dozens of pumps on display will seem a daunting task. Most good centres will have an expert to help, and if you leave the choice to the specialist it will make sense to provide some details to help.

Right, from top to bottom
1 An ultraviolet clarifier showing the hosetail connections in and out of the clarifier.

2 A submersible pump with the bonus of a ball joint connection for the outlets, making them easier to fit.

3 A combined submersible light and fountain unit conveniently secured to a base plate.

4 A powerful submersible pump suitable for continuous running with both a ball joint connection for the delivery pipe and an external strainer.

There are two terms to wrestle with at the outset: the 'head' and the 'rate of flow', as these technical phrases are fundamental to planning moving water features.

Head

The 'head' is the term used for the height that you require the pump to lift the water above the level of water in the reservoir. In the small features described in this book this is most likely to be 1–2m (3–6ft). For a fountain with a single spout of water, the 'head' is easy to understand and identify, but fountain heads with multiple or whirling sprays will need additional pressure as there are several jets each requiring pressure to the same head.

In watercourses and streams the 'head' is not to be confused with the horizontal distance that the water will travel to the top. In such a feature there would be additional loss of pressure in a long length of pipe, even though the top of the stream was only 60–90cm (2–3ft) above the water level in the bottom pool.

Rate of flow

The 'rate of flow' refers to the amount of water passing through the delivery pipe from the outlet of the pump in a given period. It is usually rated in litres

1

2

3

4

Practicalities

Buying a Pump

When you visit the aquatic centre to buy a pump, have answers to the following questions ready. The information will be invaluable for the specialist who helps you choose the best pump for your needs.

- What will the pump be used for – that is, what type of fountain or watercourse do you want?

- What are the approximate measurements of the feature?

- If you want a fountain, how high and what type of spray do you require?

- If you are planning a watercourse, what length of stream is envisaged and what size of pipe will be used? Will the water be expected to trickle or gush over the waterfalls?

- Will the pump be expected to drive more than one feature, such as a fountain and a watercourse or a fountain and a filter system?

- Do you expect to use the pump continuously or intermittently?

- If the pump is for a fish pool do you want a biological filter to help keep the water clear?

tap, allowing you to adjust the rate of water flow to suit your scheme.

The rate of flow has a significant effect on the sound. Often the fittings supplied with the pump contain a flow regulator, but when the pump is in position in the water it can be difficult to reach this control. So that you can fine tune this important aspect of your water feature, it is worth fitting a small regulating valve into the pipework at a point where it can be easily reached.

Most the pumps sold for pool features are submersible, and are submerged in a reservoir or pool to drive the moving water feature. The other type of pump, the surface pump, is positioned above the water and draws water through a suction pipe from the pool to whatever feature is required. These pumps are mainly used for larger water features than we are dealing with, but they have the advantages of slightly cheaper running costs and, because they are in a dry pump chamber above the pool, being easier to adjust or maintain than submersible pumps. They are protected from the elements by a well-ventilated pump chamber, which is built specially for the pump as close as possible to the feature itself and as near to the pool level as can be achieved.

If a pool becomes overstocked with fish and plant debris, a considerable amount of fish waste and decayed plant material will accumulate on the bottom and form an ever-increasing layer of mulm, which might eventually block a pump. A 'pondvac', which sucks out the rubbish from the bottom and disperses it through a long pipe onto the garden borders, is a useful piece of equipment. It consists of a surface pump for easy manoeuvrability, a rigid length of suction pipe with a flattened intake like a letter box and a delivery pipe. The water can be returned to the pool if required after it has passed through a holding tank, like the bag on a vacuum cleaner, where the rubbish accumulates.

or gallons per hour and is the basic guide to the pump's performance.

A simple guide to assessing the rate of flow would be to use the rate of flow from the garden hose attached to the mains water as a guideline. If you have a measure like a 9 litre (2 gallon) watering can or large bucket, measure how much water flows into the bucket or can from the hosepipe in one minute. This amount is then multiplied by 60 to calculate the rate of flow in litres (gallons) per hour.

Another rough guide to assessing how a rate of flow looks when water is passing over a waterfall stone is to bear in mind that it will take a rate of flow of 2700 litres (600 gallons) per hour to produce an unbroken sheet of water over a flat stone 15cm (6in) wide. If the 'head' is over 1m (3ft) and there is a long distance of pipe involved, this increases the rate of flow required.

Although the calibration details are shown on a curving graph on the outside of the packing box of most pumps, you may have already decided to delegate the decision on the pump size required to an expert, especially when you learn that there are further considerations, such as the friction loss in different sizes of delivery pipe, to take into account.

Choosing a pump

Most small pumps will handle a simple moving water feature that involves little more than the relatively easy task of pushing water into cobbles or circulating it through an urn. If you are in doubt, choose a pump that is more than adequate to do the job you require, and if the pump is not supplied with a flow regulating valve, buy one of these invaluable accessories. This small valve works rather like a small

FILTERS AND WATER CLARIFIERS

The small water feature, particularly a closed feature where most of the water volume is stored out of daylight and where there are no plants, should not need a sophisticated filter system. For features such as an open pool, where the surface of the water is exposed to sunshine, the problem of algae must be addressed either through the correct type of plant mixture or a filter system with or without a clarifier.

1 and 2 Two brands of ultraviolet clarifier showing the easy connections for the pipes. These clarifiers should be above water and protected from the elements.

Below Four types of biological filter showing some of the commonly used materials inside.

3 Designed to be buried with an internal pump, filtration is by gravity feed.

4 Designed for above pond use the foam sheets and plastic filter media are easy to clean.

5 A bottom-entry filter which can be buried, using gravel trays and foam in addition to the plastic filter media.

6 A three compartment filter with brushes, foam cartridges and biomedia for above-ground installation.

If the pool has no pump, the simplest system of filtration is through the plants themselves, and only when they become entirely overgrown and mulm builds up on the bottom will the pool need a complete clean out.

Even when there are a few small fish, provided there are not too many and they do not become too big, enough work is still done by the planting to keep the water clear. There is a fine point when a perfectly clear, well-balanced pool becomes cloudy and the more cloudy it gets, the less appealing it is and the more it becomes a neglected eyesore. This critical point, when the water feature can no longer sustain clear, well-oxygenated water, most commonly occurs when the pool has been made too shallow and there is insufficient shade to prevent the main volume of water from warming up quickly. The other main contributory factor is when too many or the wrong choice of fish have been introduced.

Filtration can overcome both of these conditions, but for effective filtration a pump is required, preferably a filter pump, which is capable of handling solids without a strainer on the intake of the pump. Filtration should not be regarded as a tool only necessary for the fish-keeper. There are many small water features, like still reflective pools or shallow pebble pools, where plants are not included but that still need to be kept completely clear. The pump in this instance will circulate the water through a hidden filter and clarifier without any apparent disturbance to the surface of the water. Such pools are excellent architectural features to include in small spaces and are especially effective in conservatories.

1

It is important to understand how filters works and what type would be most appropriate for your needs.

Forget the filters used in swimming pools; these are not suitable for ornamental water features. Swimming pools use chemicals and often use physical filters, which involve pumping water at pressure through tanks of sand or similar material to strain out fine particles. Ornamental pools, however, do not use chemicals – other than

2

the occasional use of algaecides when conditions necessitate such extreme short-term measures.

The filter required in an ornamental pool is one that filters out the minute green algae from the water not through the use of chemicals but through the biological action of bacteria. For the small water features described in this book there is no need to worry about big black tanks sited near the pool that are sold as biological filters. There are more aesthetic filters that can be hidden in the water, and although they are not the ideal system for the serious fish-keeper, they are perfectly adequate to ensure that the water in a small pool is clear. The water is sucked though the filter medium on

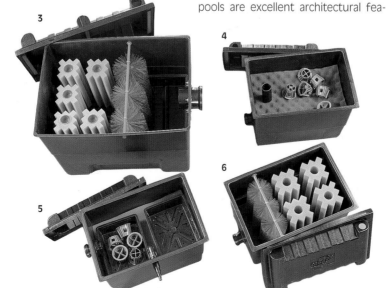

3

4

5

6

the bottom of the pool rather than being pumped through a filter above the water. The beneficial bacteria grow on the filter medium under water, and, after several weeks of water being circulated through the filter medium, they will begin to kill off the algae.

Biological filters, whether above or inside the pool, do not give instant results and they rely on constant water circulation to be effective. This is why it is important that the pump for such a filtration system should be designed for constant running rather than intermittent use, like a fountain or waterfall, and it will be necessary to run it day and night in the summer, when filtration is most required. This type of filter should not be turned on and off as the beneficial bacteria essential to killing the harmful types need some time to become established, and in areas with mild winters it may be necessary to keep the filter operating all year round because algae can grow in winter.

In the last twenty or so years, biological filtration has been supplemented by water clarifiers known as ultraviolet clarifiers (UVCs). These electrical devices work in tandem with the biological filter by exposing the circulating water to ultraviolet light as it passes through the clarifier, where there are one or two ultraviolet bulbs. These bulbs cause the minute green algae to flocculate or bunch together rather than remain solitary, making it easier for them to be collected in the filter medium of the biological filter. The bulbs are expensive and may need replacing once or twice a year, but they are extremely effective in cloudy water and very appropriate for small ornamental moving water features that rely on the water having pristine clarity.

These complex filters should not be confused with strainers, which are fitted onto most submersible pumps to prevent debris being sucked into the impellers of the pump. These simply prevent damage to the pump and will have no effect on the water clarity.

Practicalities

Water levels
It is essential to keep topping up the water level in the pool as water is lost through evaporation in hot, sunny weather or through turbulence in windy weather. Use rainwater from water butts if possible to avoid the minerals salts or chlorine in mains water. Excessive use of mains water may also cause the water to become alkaline in hard water areas, which will upset the water chemistry in the pool.

Milky water
This problem arises from the decomposition of organic matter, and a high percentage of rotting leaves and stems on the bottom is often the cause. Worse still, in a small pond or barrel there may be a dead frog or toad on the bottom, which has gone unnoticed. A good clear out is the best solution, but if this is not possible, frequent partial water changes of about one-quarter of the pond volume will help.

Left This type of heavily planted pool is unlikely to need supplementary filtration unless it is heavily stocked with fish.

FOUNTAINS

Although many of the one weekend projects are fountains in one form or another, they are not dependent on spray nozzles for the fountain head and there is seldom any open water visible in the feature. There are many different styles of fountain head available to suit any style of garden, whether classical or modern, simple or ornate.

Below The reservoir for this adaptation of the brimming urn project has been concealed under the ornamental drain cover.

The simplest spray fountains require no more than a suitable receptacle for the pool and a pump with a plastic fountain nozzle as part of the fittings. Circles or hexagons make the best open fountain pools because the fountain spray itself is circular in form, and it is important to anticipate spray drift from wind by having room on all sides to avoid water loss whatever the wind direction.

Fountains tend to be best suited to formal gardens, where they form a focal point in a symmetrical layout. The best position is often when the fountain spray is seen against the source of light and has a clear, uncluttered background. The most suitable height relates both to the diameter of the pool and to the type of spray. A wide spray, which is broken up by several fine jets of varying height, will need a clear, wide pool to provide a good setting and to catch the wispy spray so that the fountain does not lose too much water over the side in windy weather. The height of the fountain should not be greater than the diameter of the pool to be both comfortable in its setting and to contain the water in windy conditions.

Sometimes, particularly in an informal setting, the fountain need be no more than a column of water, again with the height related to the setting. The cobble fountain (see pages 54–5) is a good illustration of the single column fountain that would be spoilt if the water column was too high in relation to the height of the group of cobbles at its base. There are occasions, however, when the spout of water appears to rise from no apparent pool base and emerges from a distant shrubby or herbaceous setting. Here, as with the cobble fountain, the pool is no more than a reservoir that is covered both to prevent evaporation and to stop light entering, which would allow algae to develop. This is an idea that is exploited in many of the projects in this book and it is one of the main reasons for

the popularity of so many of the smaller water features that have no open water surface.

The fountain style and height are, therefore, related to the width and style of the garden, because this will dictate the diameter of the base pool. Because our aim in these projects is to create a fountain pool in one weekend, we cannot be too ambitious when it comes to the size of the base pool, and a raised pool with a fountain is included in the projects because it saves having to excavate the pool and fountains are particularly suited to raised surrounds.

Fountain ornaments

There is a large variety of fountain ornaments available at good garden centres, ranging from classical figures to frogs or fish with spouting mouths. Many of the free-standing ornaments sit on a separate plinth, which makes an excellent housing for the pump to sit inside. The ornaments have been manufactured with rigid pipes inside, with a flexible pipe and connector that will run between the plinth and the fountain figure.

If reaching the pump is difficult from the side of the pool when it is placed directly under the ornament, move the pump to the edge and join a flexible pipe from the pump to the connector in the plinth beneath the fountain ornament. Even though the pump may be more conspicuous, this arrangement makes it easier to alter the flow regulator and to clean the pump strainer.

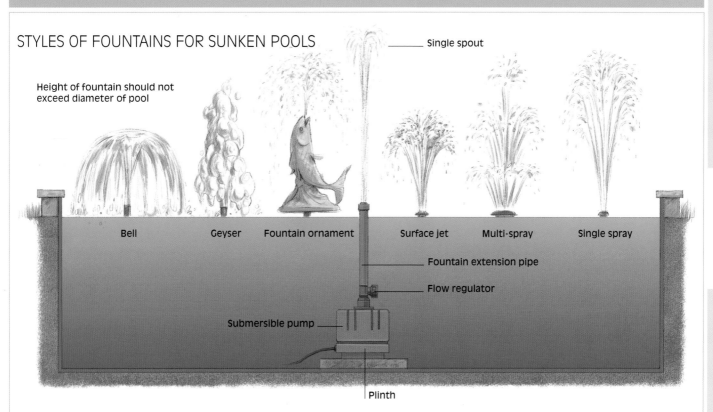

STYLES OF FOUNTAINS FOR SUNKEN POOLS

Single spout

Height of fountain should not exceed diameter of pool

Bell   Geyser   Fountain ornament   Surface jet   Multi-spray   Single spray

Fountain extension pipe

Flow regulator

Submersible pump

Plinth

Styles of fountain jet

If you install a fountain pool you may wish to explore the variety of fountain jets available, which vary considerably from the standard plastic nozzle supplied with the pump and which are available in a range of patterns.

- **Bell jet** This gives a fascinating effect in a small pool in a sheltered site. Even a gentle breeze will tend to break up the thin film of water, but it is ideal in a conservatory or in a waterlily pool where there should be no turbulence on the water surface.

- **Geyser** This produces a strong column of frothing water, which is good in a windy situation as the spray column resists

breaking up and being blown about. It requires a stronger pump than a simple spray because there are small holes in the side of the wide nozzle, which draw in air as the water rushes by, causing the frothiness of the spray. This does tend to be noisy.

- **Fountain ornaments** These are usually placed at the side or in the centre of a pool. Upright sprays are normally placed centrally whereas spouting fountains are placed at the side – making them easier to maintain.

- **Simple column** This column of water requires no more than a rigid pipe attached to the pump outlet. The skill lies in

achieving the right height and thickness of the tube of water: too narrow, and it will look too vulnerable and out of scale; too high, and it will look out of proportion. As the width of the pipe increases, so the height reduces drastically, and it needs a fairly powerful pump to achieve a column 2.5cm (1in) wide and 2m (6ft) high. It can be extremely effective in both formal and informal situations, especially when the sun strikes the column from the side.

- **Tiered fountains** These make an interesting pattern for a small garden and are simply achieved by arranging different sizes of holes in the nozzle.

Other types of fountain

A double dome is a more sophisticated form of bell jet, creating a tiered fountain inside the thin umbrella of water. It must be in a sheltered position.

In a ring fountain the spray can be directed in thin spouts from the pool perimeter inwards at an angle. A plas-

tic, semi-rigid pipe is fixed to the pool wall just above the water level, and jets are inserted into the pipe at regular intervals. A flexible pipe from the pump outlet is connected to a small spur on the circular pipe with a hose clip. The rings can be made up at specialist aquatic centres.

Rotating nozzles work in the same way as a rotating lawn sprinkler, as the water pressure forces the arms of the fountain jet to rotate quickly. The angle of the jets on the rotating arms must keep the spray pattern tight or too much water will be lost in a small fountain pool.

Wall fountains

Wall fountains have become increasingly popular as they can produce sound and movement in small spaces, and where space is particularly tight they use up no valuable ground space. They range enormously in their complexity but the project described on pages 50–1, which has a separate base pool, can be installed in one weekend. If this project is successful, you may be encouraged to make more ambitious additions and changes later, but the projects have been designed to require the minimum of building skills to achieve the maximum effect.

To create a more individual fountain than the style described on pages 50–1, you will need to find a suitable container that could stand at the bottom of the wall to act as a base pool. This could be any decorative container that is waterproof provided it has a

minimum capacity of 22–27 litres (5–6 gallons). One rather obvious suggestions for this role would be a water tank of some description, ancient or modern. The older galvanized metal tanks can often be found at builder's yards, particularly those specializing in recycling architectural items. If the tank was a more modern plastic type, this could be disguised with bushy evergreen plants such as *Buxus* spp. (box) or *Ligustrum* spp. (privet), pruned hard to form tight narrow hedge and trimmed at the top to the same level as the black tank. Alternatively, the tank sides could be rendered in a rough textured finish, like the hypertufa mix described for the glazed sink (see pages 46–7), or some sort of retaining wall could be erected with railway sleepers, timber rounds or walling stones.

This is a great opportunity to use your imagination and look for unconventional receptacles that can be adapted for the purpose. There are many containers more attractive than a tank, and it would be worth exploring large garden centres, where there is an increasing range of planters in various shapes. Many of these are quite large enough to use as base pools, especially if they are rectangular in shape so that they do not stand too high underneath the spout. Don't worry if the planters have drainage holes: these can be easily sealed with modern silicone preparations.

Don't dismiss the idea of using a small flexible liner inside a raised pool surround. Old railway sleepers make a good choice for both formal and informal gardens and you can control the height and size of the sleepers by cutting the sleepers to fit and adding height by placing one sleeper on top of the other. The edge of the liner can be disguised under a small batten tacked to the top inside edge of the top sleeper.

A semicircle is an ideal shape for a base pool under a fountain, and

Above The simplicity of the pool surround and seat is reflected in the simple elegance of the fountain.

Right Forming a surprise in a heavily planted area is one of the joys of small features like this fountain.

several models are made in self-assembly form from reconstituted stone. These make elegant surrounds, requiring no more than the placing of curved, kerb-like stones together to butt onto the existing wall. These surrounds make a shallow, raised pool, into which a flexible liner is inserted. The pre-cut liner is supplied as part of the kit, and the edge is disguised beautifully into the design of the surround.

If obtaining or building a raised pool is not possible, you can always make a sunken pool at the base of the wall as long as you are not planning the feature in a concrete yard and there is soil up to the wall. Such an arrangement offers an opportunity to use a wide choice of waterproofing materials, the easiest being a small pre-formed pool in one of the many shapes available. As with any pool, the surround of the pool will need to be considered carefully so that it matches the style of the wall, the mask and the rest of the garden. See pages 106–107 for some suggestions on ways to edge a formal pool.

Whatever type and style of base pool is chosen, you will need to insert a submersible pump into the pool, and the flexible water pipe leading from the pump to the wall spout will need to be disguised, as will the power cable to the pump. This should not be an afterthought, as leaving the mechanics visible in an otherwise imaginative creation will spoil the whole look. The wall fountain which is described on pages 50–1 suggests a suitable way of disguising the water pipe, and wherever possible you should also make room for some plants or coping to the base pool to disguise the less conspicuous power cable.

Above The strong shape of the urn means that the simple terracotta spout and piled large cobbles are all that is needed to perfect this striking composition.

The projects in this section should be within the capability of most gardeners. Many of the small water features that can be installed in a single weekend are now available in kit form, and they require little construction other than the addition of decorative materials, such as cobbles, for the surrounds.

ONE WEEKEND PROJECTS

1

One Weekend Projects

STONE SINKS AND TROUGHS

Old stone sinks and troughs can be converted successfully into miniature water gardens, provided their internal depth is at least 30cm (12in): shallower containers are better suited as alpine troughs. The main disadvantage is their weight, and it is highly unlikely that a trough could be transported in a car boot, so take transport costs and manhandling on site into account.

This project assumes that the trough or sink will sit directly on the ground rather than on brick legs, as these would require both concrete foundations and mortaring between the brick courses, and would require a second weekend's work in order to guarantee a sturdy base.

Right A small submersible pump in a reservoir under the smaller trough recirculates the water through these two troughs.

Tools & equipment

Spade

Wheelbarrow

Spirit level and long straight-
   edge

Materials

Sand

Stone trough or sink

Silicone sealant and plug if
   trough has drainage hole

Aquatic plant collection
   of 3–5 plants

1 Level the base of the site carefully and spread a 2.5cm (1in) layer of sand over it. If the trough has an uneven base standing it on a bed of sand makes levelling it easier.

2 Get help to lift the trough on to the sand base. Check that the top is level in both directions with a spirit level and straight-edge. Add sand if necessary until the trough is perfectly level.

3 If the trough has a drainage hole, use an ordinary plug and seal it with a silicone sealant. Allow the sealant to harden.

4 Partially fill the trough with water and begin planting. Include a submerged oxygenator, a plant that has striking emergent vertical leaves – *Iris laevigata* 'Variegata' or *Acorus gramineus*, for example – a plant to flop over the sides and soften the edges – *Veronica beccabunga*, *Myriophyllum aquaticum* or *Isolepis cernua*, for instance – and, if the trough is

large enough, a miniature waterlily, such as *Nymphaea* 'Pygmaea Helvola'. All these plants should be in small aquatic pots or baskets. Top up the water level.

5 To give initial shade sprinkle a few floating plants on the surface.

Practicalities

Waterproofing
Stone troughs made from soft stone, such as sandstone, may not be entirely waterproof and water will be absorbed into the stone. To avoid this, paint both the inside and outside surfaces with two coats of a proprietary water sealant.

STONE SINKS AND TROUGHS

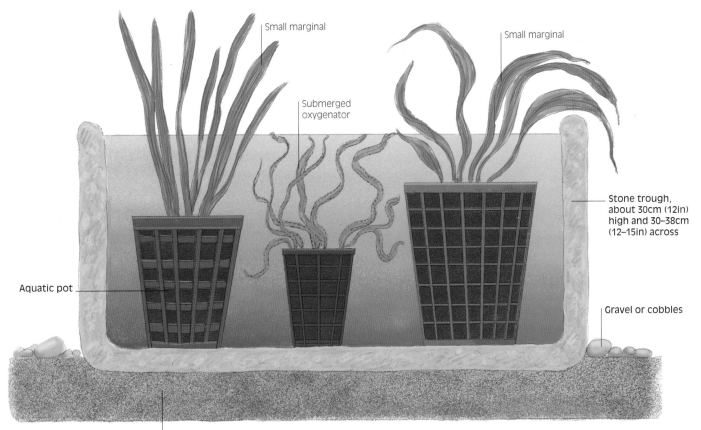

Small marginal

Submerged oxygenator

Small marginal

Stone trough, about 30cm (12in) high and 30–38cm (12–15in) across

Aquatic pot

Gravel or cobbles

Layer of sand 2.5cm (1in) deep

SIMULATED STONE SINKS AND TROUGHS

An old glazed sink can be easily converted into an attractive small water feature. If possible, place the sink on a slightly raised surface that is at a suitable working height so you do not have to bend down too much. Like the stone troughs, the sink is heavy, so you should get help when you need to lift it.

Position the sink on supports roughly 5cm (2in) thick such as narrow paving or walling stones that are just sufficient to allow the sink drain hole to clear the ground. Choose a flat site to position the sink, but you may need to use sand to get the surface properly level.

Tools & equipment

Small plasterer's trowel
Builder's wheelbarrow
Shovel
Paintbrush
Rubber gloves
Spirit level and straight-edge

Materials

Glazed sink at least 22cm (15in) deep
1 x 25kg bag of sharp sand
1 x 25kg bag of cement
1 x 40 litre bag of sphagnum peat or peat substitute
Large tin of industrial glue
Plug for drainage hole
Silicone sealant
Small collection of aquatics as recommended for the stone trough, with small aquatic planting pots and a medium-sized bag of aquatic compost

1 Clean any dirt or algae off the shiny surface of the sink with an abrasive pad such as a pan scourer. This will help the layer of hypertufa and glue to adhere better.

2 In a wheelbarrow mix thoroughly 1 part sharp sand and 1 part cement with 2 parts sphagnum peat to make up the hypertufa mix. You need sufficient materials to nearly fill a builder's wheelbarrow.

3 Paint the outer sides of the glazed sink and a generous area over both sides of the top rim with heavy-duty industrial glue.

SIMULATED STONE SINKS AND TROUGHS

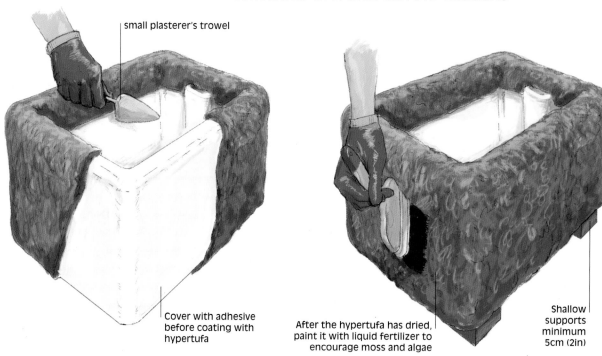

small plasterer's trowel

Cover with adhesive before coating with hypertufa

After the hypertufa has dried, paint it with liquid fertilizer to encourage moss and algae

Shallow supports minimum 5cm (2in)

4 Leave the glue to go tacky and in the meantime add a little water to the hypertufa ingredients. Mix them thoroughly to make a stiff paste.

5 Wearing a pair of strong rubber gloves, and using a small plasterer's trowel, add a small quantity of the stiff mixture, and starting at the bottom using the underside of the trowel, press small amounts of the mixture onto the sides, spreading unevenly to create as rough a texture as possible.

6 Continue adding the mix up the sides and over the rim. Leave the sink for at least 24 hours to set.

7 Make a final check that the sink is level before discarding the surplus mix. As hypertufa can chip easily when dry, avoid any unnecessary movement.

8 Insert the right-sized plug into the drainage hole and seal with a liberal quantity of waterproofing silicone sealant. Allow this to dry before partially filling the sink.

Practicalities

Drying the sink
Hypertufa must dry slowly or it will crack. If you apply it in strong sunlight, cover it with damp sacking. Frost would crack it, so cover it with polythene in frosty conditions.

9 The mix will darken and grow algae more quickly if the outside is painted with sour milk, fertilizer or a proprietary antiquing fluid.

Below This stone trough, nestling comfortably in ferns, forms a small raised pool at the base of a wall fountain.

HALF-BARRELS AND TUBS

A half-barrel or tub is an excellent way to put a stand-alone water feature in your garden. Because they are made of dark wood, they look particularly good as a feature in gravel gardens. This project assumes that the barrel is not totally watertight and will need waterproofing. If the barrel is large, you will need help to lift it into the hole.

Ideally, the barrel should be buried on a level site, leaving only 5–8cm (2–3in) of the rim sticking out. This has two advantages; first, it creates a more even water temperature, which is better for plants and fish and lessens the risk that it will be frozen solid in the winter; and second, the soil surrounding the barrel gives extra support to the hoops, which might be fragile and partly rusted.

Alternatively, if you prefer not to bury the barrel, choose a setting where the barrel looks comfortable and will be protected. If the barrel is in the middle of the garden and in full sun, the water will both evaporate more quickly and be subject to extremes of heat and cold. A sheltered corner is ideal, perhaps with a small ornament or statue at the side or, even better, another barrel or two of different sizes so that a variety of plants can surround and soften the barrels' outlines.

Tools & equipment

Spade
Spirit level and straight-edge
Wheelbarrow
Paintbrush
hammer

Right A freshly planted barrel that will soon be the centrepiece of a lush mix of hosta foliage.

Materials

Half-barrel, minimum diameter
   60cm (2ft)
Silicone sealant
Black pool waterproofing paint
Flexible liner, thin timber batten
   and tacks (as an alternative,
   see step 2)
Sand
Brick or flat stone to act as base
   for waterlily container
   (optional)
Small aquatic plant collection
   with aquatic baskets and
   aquatic compost
Bag of cobbles

1   Thoroughly clean the barrel and, if
   possible, immerse it in a tank of
   water or fill it completely with
   water for a day or two so that the
   timbers swell as much as possible.

2   Drain the barrel. Once the surface
   is dry paint the joints with silicone
   sealant. When this is dry, paint the
   inside of the barrel with black pool
   waterproofing paint, which is
   obtainable from water garden
   suppliers. This will prevent any
   chemicals from leaching into the
   water. Wait until it is thoroughly
   dry before filling the barrel.

   Alternatively, line the barrel
   with a flexible liner, holding the top
   in place with a thin timber batten
   tacked inside the barrel rim to
   disguise the liner's edge. This can
   look a little clumsy, and it is not
   easy to hide the folds of the liner
   in such a small space.

3   Invert the barrel on the ground
   and mark the outline by trickling a
   line of sand around the edge.

4   Dig the hole the same depth as the
   barrel and spread a 5–8cm (2–3in)
   layer of sand on the bottom of the
   hole. This will allow the rim of the
   barrel to project by the same
   amount above ground level.

5   Insert the barrel into the hole and
   check that it is level by laying a
   spirit level and straight-edge across
   the sides.

6   Backfill the gap between the barrel
   and the sides of the hole with soil,
   tamping it down firmly.

7   Partly fill the barrel with water and
   check the level again. If a miniature
   waterlily is to be planted, place a
   brick on the bottom of the barrel
   to elevate the planting container.

8   Plant with mixed aquatics, to
   include a submerged oxygenator
   and an erect-leaved plant, such as
   Typha minima (miniature
   reedmace) or *Iris laevigata*. To add
   interest, include *Juncus effusus*
   f. *spiralis* (corkscrew rush).

9   If you wish, you could surround
   the rim of the barrel with washed,
   rounded cobbles in order to
   disguise the edge.

HALF-BARRELS AND TUBS

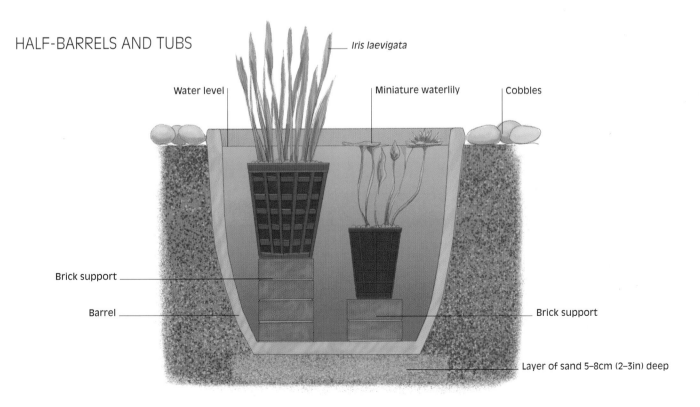

Iris laevigata

Water level

Miniature waterlily

Cobbles

Brick support

Barrel

Brick support

Layer of sand 5–8cm (2–3in) deep

One Weekend Projects

WALL FOUNTAIN WITH A SEPARATE BASE POOL

This fountain combines a lion mask for the spout and a cobble pool base, which is one of the easiest of hidden water reservoirs to construct. One of the many designs of wall trellis has been used both to frame the mask and to disguise the narrow water pipe that runs up to the back of the mask from the submersible pump that sits in the reservoir.

You may need some help to hold the trellis and battens while you fix them to the wall.

Do not build this fountain against a house wall: no matter how carefully you prepare the surface the wall will absorb water. Check the wall you are going to use to make sure that the mortar, plaster or bricks are stable.

As a precaution for times when the pressure is reduced, causing the spout to dribble rather than pour, the area of the wall under the spout should be painted with a proprietary water sealant in order to protect the surface.

Right A further refinement to hiding the delivery pipe to the wall mask has been made here in a small brick wall in front of the existing wall.

Tools & equipment

Spade
Screwdriver
Wheelbarrow
Spirit level and straight-edge
Rake
Trowel
Drill
Hacksaw
Scissors

Materials

Wall trellis and trellis surround
Wooden battens
Mask
Screws and screw fixings
Flexible corrugated plastic pipe, 19mm (¾in) in diameter and 2–3m (6–10ft) long
Copper or rigid pipe, 13mm (½in) in diameter and 8–10cm (3–4in) long, if needed
Hose clip
Plastic dustbin
Sand
Sheet of polythene, 1.2m (4ft) square
Galvanized metal grid, about 60cm (2ft) square
Submersible pump
Small paving stone to fit within bottom of reservoir
Waterproof connection socket
2–3 bags of decorative cobbles

1 Select a suitable arched or perspective trellis surround and attach a framework of battens that will support the trellis against the wall and allow a minimum gap of 2.5cm (1in) between the wall and the trellis. This allows the 13mm (½in) pipe to be threaded behind the trellis and the shoots of the plants to twine around the structure easily.

Screw the trellis to the batten framework, fixing the top of the arch as close as possible to the proposed position of the mask.

2 If the mask has no pipe to act as the spout, drill a hole through the mask to take a short length of copper pipe so that it projects slightly from the front and back.

3 Attach one end of the corrugated flexible pipe to the copper pipe at the back of the mask and use a hose clip to tighten the pipe to the copper pipe. The flexible pipe should be long enough to thread behind the trellis and reach the pump at the bottom of the reservoir.

4 Thread the flexible pipe behind the trellis so that it is hidden as much as possible and leave the loose end coiled by the wall until the reservoir is finished.

5 Stand the plastic dustbin that is to be used as the reservoir upside-down on the ground under the mask but 10cm (4in) away from the wall and mark a circle around the base with sand.

6 Dig a hole 10cm (4in) deeper than the dustbin and spread a layer of soft sand 5cm (2in) thick over the bottom of the hole.

7 Place the dustbin in the hole so that its rim is slightly below the surrounding ground level. Check that it is level by laying a spirit level on top of a straight-edge placed across the rim.

8 Rake out a shallow, saucer-shaped depression, about 1.2m (4ft) across, in the soil around the dustbin so that the bottom of the 'saucer' is level with the top of the dustbin. Place a piece of polythene across this depression and cut a hole in the polythene above the dustbin. The hole must be slightly smaller in diameter than the top of the dustbin.

9 To check the fit, place the galvanized metal grid on top of the polythene so that it rests on the rim of the dustbin beneath.

10 Remove the grid and place the pump in the bottom of the dustbin so that it sits on a plinth, such as a piece of broken paving slab. Thread the loose end of the flexible pipe through the grid, connect it to the pump outlet and replace the grid. Thread the pump cable under the grid and connect it to a nearby waterproof socket or switch.

11 Half-fill the dustbin with water and check the level again. Turn on the pump. Any adjustments to the rate of flow from the spout can be made at this stage by altering the flow regulator on the outlet attachment of the pump.

12 If everything is working satisfactorily, add more water, filling the reservoir to about 8cm (3in) from the top. Arrange cobbles over the grid and surrounding polythene. Cut off any pipe protruding from the mask with a hacksaw.

13 Plant climbing plants near the base of the trellis.

14 If you wanted to make the base pool more formal at a later stage, you could edge the cobbles with a semi-circular brick surround.

WALL FOUNTAIN WITH A SEPARATE BASE POOL

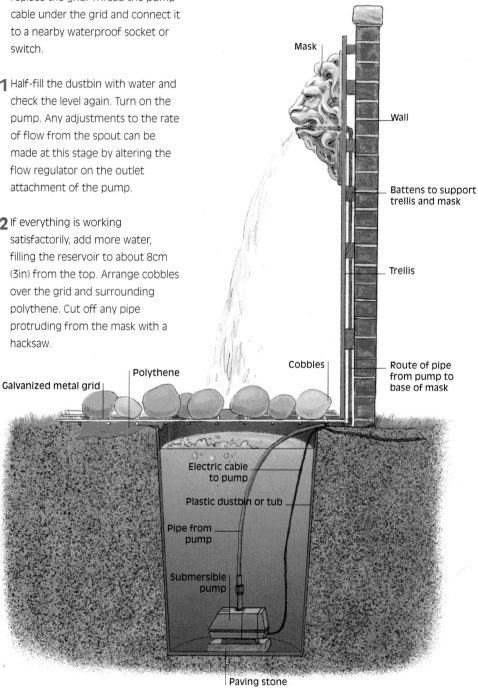

Mask

Wall

Battens to support trellis and mask

Trellis

Cobbles

Route of pipe from pump to base of mask

Polythene

Galvanized metal grid

Electric cable to pump

Plastic dustbin or tub

Pipe from pump

Submersible pump

Paving stone

RAISED POOL WITH A SPRAY FOUNTAIN

The pool used in this project is a standard pattern available from most of the large garden timber manufacturers, and it is supplied on a self-assembly basis: the sides interlock and are secured with screws. Surrounded by soft planting and small shrubs, it is a relatively easy way to introduce a stylish water feature into the garden.

The timbers are normally pressure treated, and reputable suppliers will give good guarantees. A flexible liner, made to measure for the pool, is often supplied with the kit. The pump is normally not supplied with these pools, allowing you to choose the size of pump and type of fountain spray.

Because the liner forms the bottom of the pool – there is no timber base supplied – it is essential that the site is perfectly flat.

Tools & equipment

Spade or rake if the pool is to be
    installed on soil that may not
    be level
Hammer
Spirit level and straight-edge
Screwdriver
Hacksaw

Right The planting has cleverly disguised and softened the outline of this raised pool with an excellent mix of evergreen foliage and bright summer flowers.

RAISED POOL WITH A SPRAY FOUNTAIN

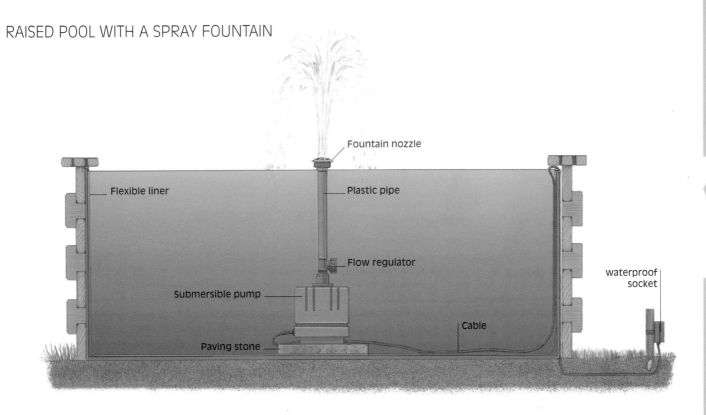

Fountain nozzle

Flexible liner

Plastic pipe

Flow regulator

Submersible pump

waterproof socket

Paving stone

Cable

Materials

Pool self-assembly kit
Securing screws (if not supplied)
Sand
Submersible pump
Small paving stone

1   Measure one long and one short side of the kit. Mark out with sand a rectangle of this size on the ground. Level out this area and make sure that all stones and roots that might damage the liner are removed.

2   Assemble the sides and secure them with the screws into the pre-marked positions. Check that the sides are level in both directions with a spirit level and straight-edge. The assembled pool is light enough to be moved into place so you can check if any adjustments are necessary to level the ground.

3   Drape the liner supplied with the kit inside the pool. To secure the edges above the waterline, the liner is stapled or tacked to the underside of the top timber overhang. The edge of the liner will be hidden under the overhang.

4   Place the pump in the centre of the empty pool on a small paving slab so that the pump cannot suck in any debris that later accumulates on the pool bottom.
    Before you fill the pool with water, thread the pump cable over the edge of the liner and between the outside of the liner and the inside of the timber surround. Pull it out from the bottom of the pool surround by lifting the pool. Connect the remaining length of cable to a nearby waterproof switch or connector.

5   The fountain jet will need to be above the water level. A length of rigid plastic pipe is supplied with most fountain kits to fit on the pump and to extend above the water level.
    The fountain nozzle is fitted into the top end of this rigid pipe. If it is too high, cut the pipe to just above water level with a hacksaw. If it is too short, the pump can be elevated in the pool with one or two bricks underneath the pump. Do not raise the pump so high that it is too close to the surface, or air will be sucked into it.

6   Fill the pool with water and turn on the pump. Make adjustments to the force and height of the fountain by altering and trying out the flow regulator on the outlet of the pump.

COBBLE FOUNTAIN

This project makes the fountain from individual items rather than from a kit, and one reason for this is to give a larger reservoir than is available with many of the kits now available. Although most self-assembly kits make it possible to install a water feature where the need for building skills may otherwise be a deterrent, this project requires little skill and little more time to complete than a kit would need.

On a patio, where the fountain is surrounded by paving, the feature will look more interesting if there is room to remove the paving for the fountain in an irregular pattern rather than just taking up a square of one or more slabs. Even though only a small part of the removed paving is necessary for the fountain jet, if there are plants or other cobbles in the area just beyond the fountain spout, the feature will blend into its surroundings more successfully. A cobble fountain can be incorporated in areas well beyond a patio: a gravel area, an island bed in the lawn or a small border are potential sites that would add individuality to a garden.

Tools & equipment

Spade

Rake

Trowel

Scissors

Wheelbarrow

Spirit level and straight-edge

Hacksaw

Right Small pieces of limestone rock add height and variety to the layer of cobbles in this fountain, which has been inserted into an existing patio.

Materials

Plastic dustbin

Soft sand

Sheet of heavy-duty polythene, 3m (10ft) square

Submersible pump with rigid or flexible extension pipe for outlet, about 45cm (18in) long

Small paving stone to fit in bottom of reservoir

Galvanized metal mesh, 60–75cm (24–30in) square, with a mesh smaller than the cobbles or pebbles

3–4 bags of mixed washed cobbles

1 Mark the size of the hole by inverting the plastic dustbin and marking around its rim with sand.

2 Dig out a hole 10cm (4in) deeper than the dustbin. This will let the dustbin rim sit below soil level.

3 Spread a layer of soft sand, 5cm (2in) deep, over the bottom of the hole and place the dustbin in the hole. Check it is level with a spirit level and straight-edge.

4 Backfill sifted soil or sand around the sides of the bin and tamp it down firmly. Use a rake to make a shallow, saucer-shaped depression in the soil, extending about 1m (3ft) outside the rim of the dustbin and up to the existing soil level.

5 Drape the polythene over the hole and surrounding area. Cut a hole in the polythene above the dustbin and slightly smaller than the diameter of the bin.

6 Check the mesh fits by placing it on the bin. The mesh should rest on the rim and be strong enough to support the weight of cobbles.

7 Remove the mesh and place the pump in the bottom of the bin, resting it on a piece of paving slab so that the pump intake is above any debris that might accumulate. Thread the pump cable and a length of rigid or flexible pipe from the pump outlet through the mesh above. Replace the mesh and hold the spirit level against the side of the rigid pipe to check that the it is completely vertical as it emerges from the mesh.

8 Partly fill the bin with water and check again that it is level. Connect the pump cable to a waterproof switch or socket and turn on the pump. If the spout is too high, make any adjustment to the flow adjuster on the pump outlet.

9 When you are happy with the rate of flow, check that the rigid pipe is protruding at the right height through the mesh to allow it to be surrounded with and disguised by cobbles. If it is too high, cut off some pipe with a hacksaw. If it is only a little too low, elevate the pump slightly in the reservoir by adding another paving stone. After making any alterations check that the pipe is returned to a true vertical position.

10 Fill the reservoir and cover the polythene and mesh with cobbles. Do not use small cobbles that will fall through the mesh. Turn on the pump and make any final adjustments to the arrangement of the cobbles around the spout.

COBBLE FOUNTAIN

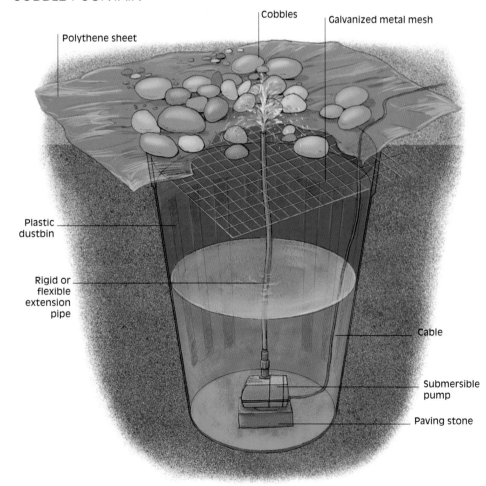

Polythene sheet

Cobbles

Galvanized metal mesh

Plastic dustbin

Rigid or flexible extension pipe

Cable

Submersible pump

Paving stone

MILLSTONE FOUNTAIN

Similar to the simple cobble fountain, the millstone fountain uses the same basic principle of a closed reservoir below ground level, with the pumped water falling back into it. The water spills from the centre of the simulated millstone, spreading in a thin moving film over the top and sides and finally falling back into the reservoir below.

This project uses a millstone kit, because the simulated millstone, which is made of fibreglass, has a sandblasted surface that looks extremely realistic but is in fact very light in weight. A real or reconstituted millstone of the same size would not only be very difficult to lift but, more importantly, would also require an extremely strong support when it was placed over the reservoir. The millstone will not require such a large catchment area for spray as the cobble fountain if it is in a windy site, so it can be tucked into more positions in the garden than the latter, including sloping sites.

Tools & equipment

Spade
Wheelbarrow
Spirit level and straight-edge
Small piece of paving stone

Right
The flat surface of the millstone fountain makes an ideal addition to this informal mix of paving slabs and gravel.

MILLSTONE FOUNTAIN

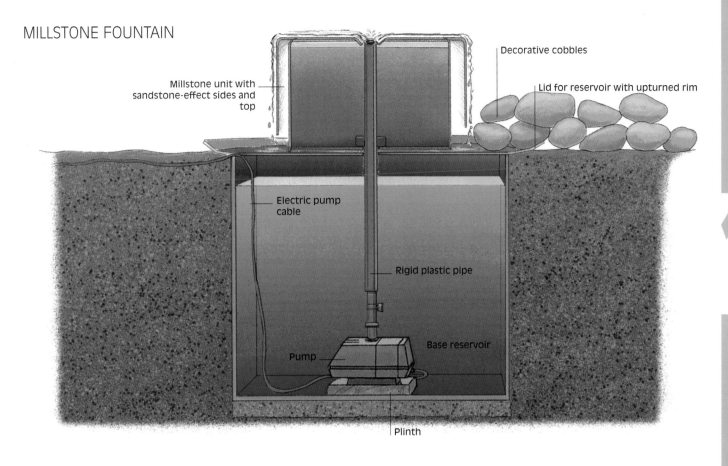

Millstone unit with sandstone-effect sides and top

Decorative cobbles

Lid for reservoir with upturned rim

Electric pump cable

Rigid plastic pipe

Base reservoir

Pump

Plinth

Materials

Millstone kit (a reservoir about 60cm (2ft) in diameter and 30cm (1ft) deep; a top for the reservoir that will support the weight of the millstone but allow the water back into the reservoir; the millstone itself, about 45cm (18in) in diameter and 23cm (9in) deep; and a short length of rigid plastic pipe, 15cm (6in) long and 13mm (½in) in diameter)

Soft sand

Submersible pump

Bag of mixed cobbles to surround the millstone

1 Place the reservoir on the soil in the position of the millstone and mark the outline with sand.

2 Dig a hole the same diameter and 5cm (2in) deeper than the reservoir.

3 Spread 5cm (2in) of sand over the bottom of the hole and replace the reservoir. Check that it is level with a spirit level and straight-edge.

4 Place the pump in the centre of the reservoir on a shallow plinth, such as a piece of paving stone 2.5–5cm (1–2in) deep.

5 Attach the rigid tube to the pump outlet.

6 Place the lid on top of the reservoir with its central hole over the rigid tube.

7 Lay the millstone on top of the reservoir lid so that the top of the rigid tube is just below level of the rim of the central hole in the millstone.

8 Use the spirit level and straight-edge to check that the top of the millstone is absolutely level. The slightest discrepancy will cause the water to flow to one side instead of evenly over the top.

9 Turn on the pump and make any necessary alterations to the flow adjuster or the levels in order to obtain a satisfactory amount of water that will form a thin film over the millstone.

10 As a finishing touch, place some washed cobbles of various sizes around the millstone sides so that the fountain harmonizes with its surroundings.

BRIMMING URN

The introduction of so many new shapes, sizes and colour shades of terracotta pots and urns has encouraged garden designers to experiment with the shapes to make moving water features. One of the most successful of these is the brimming urn, which enhances the curving shapes and rim of the urns with a thin film of overflowing water that glistens in the sunshine.

The urn can be sited almost anywhere in the garden, from plant borders, to patios and raised beds, and these features look particularly appealing when they are caught in low sunshine. You should take strict precautions in providing a very sturdy and solid base for what will be a large, heavy urn full of water.

Above The brimming urn becomes a focal point in the garden, allowing a variety of similar shapes and sizes of container to be grouped nearby.

Tools & equipment

Spade
Trowel
Wheelbarrow
Rake
Wirecutters
Paintbrush
Spirit level
Electric drill

Materials

Ornamental urn
Flexible liner, about 2m (6ft)
    square
1 x 25kg bag of soft sand
1 x 25kg bag of ready-mixed
    cement
About 12 bricks
Galvanized metal grid, about
    60cm (2ft) square
Plastic-coated wire
Mastic or silicone sealant
Length of copper pipe, 13mm
    (½in) in diameter, slightly
    longer than the urn
Tank coupler (optional; see
    step 9)
Hose clip and 19mm (¾in) plastic
    flexible pipe, 1m (3ft) long

1   Select the site and check that the ground is soft enough to dig a hole for the reservoir, which should be a minimum of 75cm (30in) in diameter and 35cm (14in) deep. Dig out the hole and rake the bottom to remove any sharp stones. Spread a 5cm (2in) layer of sand over the base of the hole.

2   Drape a flexible liner into the excavation, making sure that there is a slight overlap at the sides. Hold the overlap down temporarily by placing bricks or cobbles on the edges of the liner.

3   Place the urn in the hole and mark the outline on the liner with sand.

4   Add a small quantity of water to enough of the ready-mixed concrete to give a stiff layer, about 2.5cm (1in) thick, that will cover the outline of the urn base on the liner. Place a large paving stone or enough smaller stones to cover the concrete mix and tap them down level. Use a spirit level to make sure the stone or stones are perfectly level.

5   Build up three piers of bricks in a triangular shape to just above the level of the top of the reservoir. Check the level by placing a spirit level and straight-edge across the sides of the reservoir hole. Shallow columns of bricks can be held together with mastic or builder's adhesive, but deeper columns

must be mortared (see practicalities). If possible, there should be enough room to house the small submersible pump between the brick piers. If there is not enough space, the pump can be housed nearer the side of the reservoir. When the top brick is reached, use a spirit level and straight-edge to check that the three piers are level.

6 Place a galvanized metal mesh over the excavation so that it rests on the sides of the hole and is supported by the brick piers in the centre.

7 Place the urn on the piers to check that the mesh does not affect its rigidity or level. Use wirecutters to cut out any parts of the mesh that cause the urn to be unstable and also cut out a small square in the mesh and hinge this square with plastic-coated wire so that you can install or remove the pump without having to remove the whole mesh.

8 Remove the urn and, if there is no drainage hole, make a hole in the bottom of the urn by drilling with a slow-speed drill; the hole should be wide enough to accommodate a 13mm (½in) copper pipe.

9 There are two ways to introduce the water through the bottom of the urn. The easiest is to push a copper pipe through the hole that has just been created until it almost reaches the top rim of the urn, leaving sufficient pipe underneath to connect to a flexible pipe from the pump. The point where the pipe goes through the drainage hole is sealed with a mastic or silicone sealant. The alternative method involves fitting a water tank coupler, available from a builder's

merchants. This fits around the hole on both sides and allows a pipe to be fitted or dismantled easily on each side of the coupler. This has the advantage that the whole assembly of pipes and pump can be dismantled more easily if necessary. It is important to have the top of the internal pipe inside the urn as high as possible. If the pipe is lowered, quite large quantities of water will drain back into the reservoir causing it to overflow and leading to serious water loss every time the pump is turned off.

10 Whatever method is used in step 9, connect the pump to the rigid pipe protruding from the bottom of the urn by a flexible pipe slightly larger than the copper pipe and secured with a hose clip. The reservoir and urn can now be filled with water.

Practicalities

Supporting larger urns
This project uses a relatively small urn. For a larger urn, which will need a wider and deeper reservoir, the bricks should be mortared between the courses for stability and strength. This means that you should allow two weekends so that the mortar has time to set properly.

11 Connect and turn on the pump, making any changes to the flow regulator on the pump to achieve an even flow of water over the sides. Avoid creating too much of a spout above the rim of the urn because this can be caught by the wind and cause extra water loss.

12 Cover the grid above the reservoir with cobbles. When it is used for long periods in hot weather, top up the reservoir so it does not dry out and damage the pump.

BRIMMING URN

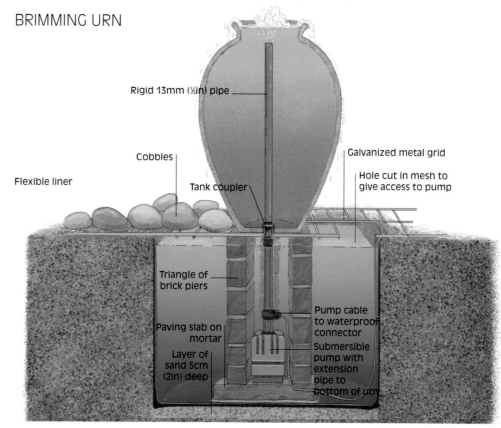

Rigid 13mm (½in) pipe

Cobbles

Flexible liner

Tank coupler

Galvanized metal grid

Hole cut in mesh to give access to pump

Triangle of brick piers

Paving slab on mortar

Layer of sand 5cm (2in) deep

Pump cable to waterproof connector

Submersible pump with extension pipe to bottom of urn

DRILLED ROCK FOUNTAIN

Continuing the theme of cobbles, millstones and urns being used in fountains where the water simply falls back into a hidden reservoir, individual rock pieces can be used to make an attractive focal point. The rugged form of the rock means that the water will play over it in different ways, creating different effects.

Below A large rock, often inconspicuous at the bottom of a rock pile, becomes a sculpture in its own right when used as a drilled fountain.

Several types of rock look very impressive when treated as specimens, and the rock surface is enhanced by the sheen of water. Buy them ready-drilled.

The larger rocks or cobbles will be heavier than a standard cobble fountain, and the grid support over the reservoir may need reinforcing. Because the level of the grid is not quite as critical as it is in the millstone or brimming urn projects (see pages 56–7 and 58–9), metal bars under the grid are easier to install than brick piers as described for the brimming urn.

Tools & equipment

Spade
Wheelbarrow
Wirecutters
Wire

Materials

Drilled rock or boulder
Galvanized metal grid, 60–90cm
    (2–3ft square), depending on
    the size of the rock
Two metal bars if the rock is
    heavy
Small bag of soft sand
Rigid or flexible liner (see step 2)
4 bricks
Short length of flexible pipe,
    19mm (¾in) or 13mm (½in) in
    diameter and about 60cm (2ft)
    long (the larger diameter pipe
    will be necessary if the
    narrower fails to lodge in the
    rock successfully)
Hose clip and short length of
    copper pipe (to gain a more
    secure fitting into the rock)
Piece of paving stone
Galvanized wire

DRILLED ROCK FOUNTAIN

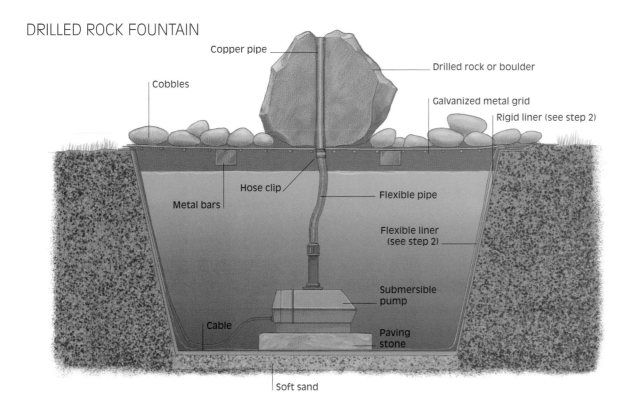

Copper pipe

Cobbles

Drilled rock or boulder

Galvanized metal grid

Rigid liner (see step 2)

Hose clip

Metal bars

Flexible pipe

Flexible liner (see step 2)

Submersible pump

Cable

Paving stone

Soft sand

1 Depending on the size of rock or boulder, dig out a roughly square or circular hole, which will later act as a reservoir for the pump. For most rocks, the hole needs to be 60–90cm (2–3ft) in diameter and 30–38cm (12–15in) deep. These dimensions can be no more than a guide, and the reservoir can be smaller if you are prepared to top up the water very regularly, especially in warmer weather. A larger reservoir gives leeway for a little neglect.

2 Line the base of the hole with a 2.5–5cm (1–2in) layer of sand and insert either a rigid liner or a flexible liner, which has been measured to fit the hole. (When measuring for flexible liners to fit excavations, add twice the depth of the hole to the measurements for the bottom then add a few centimetres (inches) for overlapping.) Hold down the edges

of the liner temporarily with stones or bricks until the installation is finished.

3 Place the pump on a small paving stone in the bottom of the hole and attach some flexible hose, 60–75cm (24–30in) long, to the delivery outlet. Leave the open end to attach to the rock later.

4 Place two tubular metal rods across the hole, supporting them on the opposite sides on bricks. These will give additional support for a heavy rock. Place a galvanized metal grid, larger than the diameter of the hole, on top of the metal rods. If the rock or boulder is small, the galvanized metal grid will be adequate support on its own.

5 Cut a section of the grid with wirecutters and make a hinge with wire to form an access window into the reservoir so that you can

adjust or remove the pump. Place the rock on the grid and thread the open end of the flexible pipe from the pump through the grid. Wedge it into the hole at the bottom of the rock. If the flexible pipe will not stay in the hole, push a small length of rigid pipe, such as copper pipe, into the hole and attach the hose to this, securing it with a hose clip.

6 Half-fill the reservoir and turn on the pump. Adjust the flow rate.

7 Top up the water in the reservoir and cover the remaining area of the grid with cobbles to disguise the grid and the edges of the liner.

JAPANESE WATER FEATURES

The rituals of the Japanese tea ceremony led to the development of the *tsukubai*, which consists of a hollowed-out stone basin constantly filled with water. This was traditionally used for washing the hands before entering the tea house. The *shishi odoshi* is a modern take on the same idea.

In order to make the visitor stoop in humility to use the vessel, it was also traditional for the height of the basin to be no more than 20–30cm (8–12in).

The tsukubai *has become a popular ornamental water feature in many Western gardens, where, although completely losing its cultural connotations, it still provides a fascinating addition to the oriental-style garden.*

The tsukubai *is an ideal water feature for a small, shady and sheltered corner where the planting is kept simple and where moss and algae can accumulate on the constantly wet basin. To achieve the subtle balance between the existing garden and features like the* tsukubai *or* shishi odoshi, *they should be integrated with care. With the exception of evergreen azaleas, flowering plants are not important in the overall scheme of a Japanese garden. Plants such as bamboos and* Acer palmatum *(Japanese maple) are more often chosen for their stems and their leaf colour.*

JAPANESE WATER FEATURE

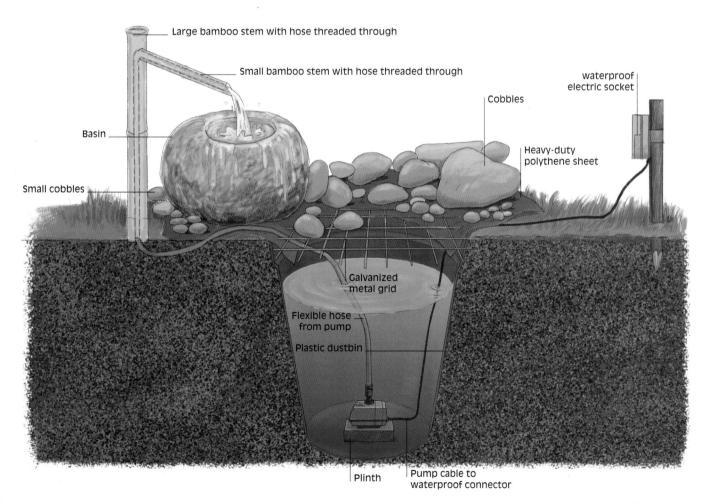

Large bamboo stem with hose threaded through

Small bamboo stem with hose threaded through

Cobbles

waterproof electric socket

Basin

Heavy-duty polythene sheet

Small cobbles

Galvanized metal grid

Flexible hose from pump

Plastic dustbin

Plinth

Pump cable to waterproof connector

Tools & equipment

Spade
Rake
Wheelbarrow
Trowel
Scissors
Spirit level and straight-edge
Drill with bits for wood drilling
Hacksaw

Materials

Plastic dustbin
Heavy-duty polythene, 60–90cm
    (2–3ft) square
Sand
Galvanized metal grid, about
    60cm (2ft) square
Stone basin
2–3 bags of rounded cobbles
2 lengths of bamboo cane, one
    with a minimum diameter of
    8cm (3in) and one with a
    diameter of 5cm (2in)
Plastic pipe, 13mm (½in) in
    diameter and about 2m (6ft)
    long
Submersible pump
Colourless adhesive
2 bamboo canes, each about 2m
    (6ft) long (optional)

1 Dig a hole and insert a plastic
dustbin, following the steps
outlined for a cobble fountain on
pages 54–5. Use a rake to create a
shallow, saucer-shaped depression
around the hole.

2 Place a sheet of heavy-duty
polythene across the depression
and cut a hole in the polythene
above the dustbin, slightly smaller
than the diameter of the dustbin.
Place a galvanized metal grid on
top of the polythene so that it is
supported on the top edge of the
dustbin. Use a spirit level and
straight-edge to check it is level.

3 Place a hollowed-out, basin-shaped
piece of rock on the polythene
sheet just outside the rim of the
dustbin. Wedge small stones or
cobbles underneath one side of
the basin so that when it is full, the
water will spill out on the side
nearest the hole in the polythene.

4 Arrange a group of cobbles beside
the slightly raised side of the basin
to help support a length of
bamboo stem in an upright
position. This upright bamboo
stem should have a minimum
external diameter of about 8cm
(3in) and be about 23cm (9in)
higher than the basin. Ream out
the insides of both bamboo canes
so that a plastic pipe can be
pushed through them.

5 Cut a circular hole about 5cm (2in)
from the top of the stem. The hole
should be large enough for you to
wedge the smaller bamboo stem
at a slightly sloping angle towards
the basin. The external diameter of
this second piece need be no more
than the width required to push a
flexible plastic pipe through the
bamboo, and long enough to spill
the water into the basin. Secure
the joint of the two pipes with
colourless, waterproof adhesive.

6 Push a flexible plastic pipe through
both pipes, hiding the open end
just inside the smaller, sloping pipe.
Connect the other end to the
pump. If necessary, arrange two
bamboo canes at an angle to form
a V-shaped support for the
bamboo spout.

7 Half-fill the reservoir with water
and check the flow of the pump,
making any alterations to the flow
regulator as required.

8 Top up the water in the reservoir
and cover the grid with cobbles.

Shishi odoshi

Another feature using bamboo cane
as a water outlet is the *shishi odoshi*
or deer scarer, which was devised by
Japanese farmers to ward off wild
animals with an intermittent clicking
noise, created when a hinged length
of bamboo cane strikes a stone. It
works on the same principle as the
tsukubai, with water from a sunken
reservoir pumped though a pipe that
is concealed within a vertical 'post' of

hollowed-out bamboo. This 'post' is connected to a thinner, hollowed-out spout that is set near the top of the post through which the water runs out. To create the clicking noise, a hole is cut halfway up the 'post', where another length of bamboo is set in order to pivot on an axle.

This piece of bamboo is hollowed out only as far as its first node, so that the heavier, opposite end falls under its own weight to strike a stone specially positioned beneath it. The hollower, lighter end lies beneath the spout to receive water pouring from it. The weight of the water accumulating in the hollowed section eventually overbalances the pipe, the water runs out, the pipe swings back up and the far end strikes the stone as it falls.

The *shishi odoshi,* with its more complex construction of a pivoting arm, is more difficult to make than a *tsukubai,* and you will probably want to use a ready-assembled kit, which requires no more fixing than connecting the flexible 13mm (½in pipe). The setting for the *shishi odoshi* can be the same as the *tsukubai,* requiring a basin or cobble base. The main essential is to ensure that the pivoting pipe, which causes the part of the bamboo stem to click against a hard object when it empties, is positioned so that the stem catches the side of the hollowed-out basin or a rock placed on the cobble grid.

Above An intriguing mix of textures where the deer scarer seems all the more mysterious because there is no obvious source of water.

The projects described here are, necessarily, larger in both scale and aspiration than the smaller features that can be constructed in a single weekend. Nevertheless, all these features are well within the capabilities of the amateur gardener.

TWO WEEKEND PROJECTS

WILDLIFE POOL

All pools with an open water surface will attract wildlife, and the more diverse the surroundings, the greater the variety of wildlife that will be attracted, but such pools need be no larger than the dimensions needed to maintain a healthy biological balance in the water. The main requirements are a design and planting scheme sympathetic to the needs of the creatures you want to visit your garden.

Site the pool where it can be seen without it being so close to the house that visiting birds become nervous. Try to surround the pool with an informal setting and ample cover of mixed evergreen and deciduous shrubs. This pool has a layer of soil on top of the liner in order to provide a submerged habitat for more creatures in the mud. A pool without a soil layer can be made following the directions for an informal pool on pages 76–9, provided that one part of the pool side has a shallow edge. An oval pool works well for this type of construction, and one with a rough size no longer than 3m (9ft) and no wider than 2m (6ft) should be possible to excavate, line and plant in two weekends.

Tools & equipment

Hosepipe, string or sand for marking out
Half-moon edging tool (if the pool is sited in a lawn)
Wooden pegs, about 2.5cm (1in) in diameter and 15cm (6in) long
Hammer
Spirit level and straight-edge, about 2m (6ft) long
Spade
Wheelbarrow
Rake
Secateurs
Scissors
Bricks or heavy stones
Piece of paving slab

Materials

Underlay
Flexible liner
Plants
Boulders, large cobbles or rocks

1   Mark out the outline of the pool with sand, string or a hosepipe. Wildlife pools are more effective in informal settings, so make the pool outline an informal shape.

2   To ensure that the pool is level, knock in flat-topped pegs around its outline about 1m (3ft) apart. Knock in one peg to the level that you require as the finished pool level; this peg will be referred to as the datum peg. Using a spirit level and a straight-edge to check the levels of the top of the pegs, knock in the other pegs to the same height as the datum peg.

3   Now start digging out the pool. Even a relatively small pool produces quite a large heap of soil, and if you have no plans for using it in the existing garden, you will have to hire a small skip to remove it. Keep the excavated topsoil separate from the subsoil because some of it will be needed to form a base layer in the pool. The cross-section of the pool will be bowl-like in shape with a shallow rim at the edge. The slope of the bowl needs to be so shallow that soil will remain on the sides of the bowl

Right An absolute oasis for wildlife with a closely planted lush mix acting as a magnet to a huge variety of creatures and insects.

Opposite Although a true wildlife pool will be dominated by indigenous plants, as long as there are shallow edges and thick planting, the pool will soon be seething with life.

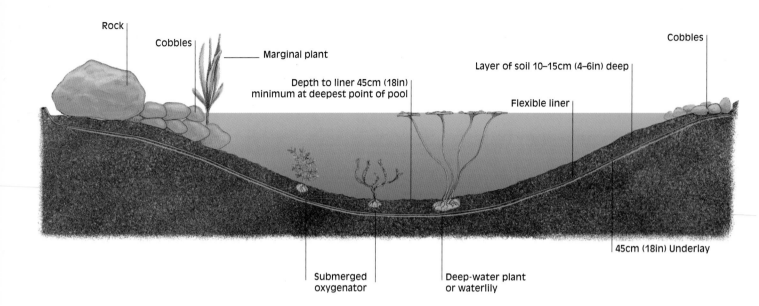

Rock

Cobbles

Marginal plant

Depth to liner 45cm (18in)
minimum at deepest point of pool

Layer of soil 10–15cm (4–6in) deep

Cobbles

Flexible liner

Submerged
oxygenator

Deep-water plant
or waterlily

45cm (18in) Underlay

Practicalities

Brown water

The most likely cause of brown water in a pool is the constant stirring up of mud on the bottom by fish. Small lined ponds that do not have deliberately introduced soil on the bottom are unlikely to experience this condition unless mud has been allowed to build up over the years and fish like koi, which explore the sediment, have been introduced. The brown colouring is not harmful, and in a wildlife pool it will make the inhabitants less nervous than crystal clear water. The colouring is caused by fine inorganic particles in suspension in the water, and it can be helped by chemicals known as flocculating agents. These cause the fine particles to clump together and sink to the bottom more readily. Flocculating agents are not algaecides, and when you ask for the product at a retailer, make sure that the supplier gives you the correct one. The problem will recur, however, if nothing is done to prevent the mud being constantly disturbed.

and not slump to the bottom. The deepest part of the bowl should be 45cm (18in), which means that the pool needs a larger surface area than a pool of the same depth with vertical side walls.

4 When you have dug the hole, rake over the sides to remove stones or other objects with sharp edges. Use secateurs to cut off exposed roots neatly. Build up low edges with soil or remove mounds around the sides so that the perimeter of the pool is level with the pegs.

5 Drape a sheet of underlay into the excavation. Overlapping rolls may be necessary in a larger pool.

6 Lay the flexible liner in the hole and temporarily secure the edge with stones or bricks.

7 Sift the topsoil you excavated from the hole to remove all stones and use it to cover the liner completely with a layer 10–15cm (4–6in) deep.

8 Use a hosepipe to begin to fill the pool gently, resting the hose outlet on a paving slab so that the force of the water does not disturb the fresh soil.

9 As the water reaches its final level, remove the pegs and trim away the excess liner, leaving sufficient to bury under soil or rocks around the pool. Before you trim away any excess liner above the finished water level, make absolutely certain that there is adequate liner around the whole perimeter.

10 Throw bunches of oxygenating plants into the deeper area. These will root quickly into the mud. See pages 134–5 on the number required for the surface area of your pool.

11 Get help with planting a deep-water plant such as a waterlily in a planting basket. So that you do not disturb the fresh mud, this is best achieved by threading two long strings through the top layer of mesh on each side of the planting basket. Two people hold the ends of the strings on opposite sides of the pool and lower the basket gently into position.

12 Young marginals can be planted in the shallower sides. Kneel at the pool side and plant as far into the mud as far as you can reach without standing in the mud.

13 Position rounded stones or boulders at random around the sides to provide shelter for amphibians.

14 Throw some native free-floating plants on the surface.

Above Flat-topped rocks make ideal platforms for amphibians, which may also hibernate under them.

REFLECTIVE POOL

As well as the mirror image of surrounding garden features in the surface of the water, this pool has the advantage of minimizing the unsightly gap between the water surface and the surrounding edge, a gap that both exposes large areas of liner to sunlight and reduces the impact of the water surface, making it more difficult to see from a distance.

This pool is about 2.4m (8ft) square, and is edged by 60cm (2ft) paving slabs. On sandy and loose soils it would be better if the pool sides were built with an edge of concrete blocks to give extra stability. However, this would take more than two weekends, and so this project assumes that the soil is quite firm enough to hold the paving.

1 Mark out the site for the square pool with string. Check that the corners are at right angles, using a builder's square in each corner and measuring to ensure that the four sides are identical in length.

2 It is essential that the sides are perfectly level for a brimming pool, so knock in pegs in the corners and two intermediate pegs along each side, about 80cm (30in) apart. Starting at one corner, knock in the peg to the level of the top of the paving that will surround the pool. Knock in the adjacent peg so that its top is level with the first corner peg. Use a spirit level to make sure that the second peg is level with the corner peg, continue to work round the square, making all the peg tops level.

Tools & equipment

Spade
Rake
Wheelbarrow
String
Builder's square
Plasterer's trowel
Watering can
Spirit level and straight-edge, about 1m (3ft) long
Extending metal tape measure
Secateurs
Scissors
Lump hammer
Craft knife

Materials

Pegs, about 2.5cm (1in) in diameter and 23cm (9in) long
4 x 25kg bags of soft sand
2 x 25kg bags of ready-mixed mortar
20 square paving slabs, each 60cm (2ft) square
Underlay
Flexible liner, about 5m (17ft) square
Plants

REFLECTIVE POOL

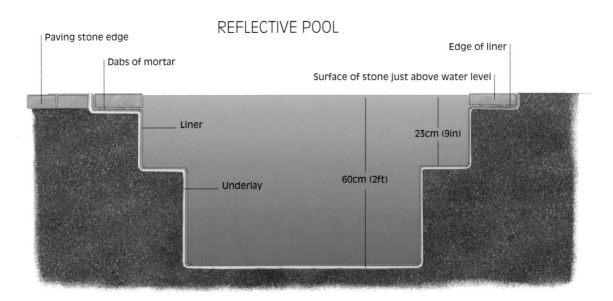

Paving stone edge

Dabs of mortar

Edge of liner

Surface of stone just above water level

Liner

23cm (9in)

Underlay

60cm (2ft)

3 Begin digging out the soil to a depth of 23cm (9in). If the soil is light and unstable, stop the sides falling away by sloping them at an angle of no more than 20 degrees. The topsoil can be spread on the garden borders or stored for future use. If stored, keep it separate from the subsoil.

4 Once the pool outline has been dug out to 23cm (9in) all over, use sand to mark the deep area of the pool, which will need another 37cm (15in) of soil excavated. The areas left at 23cm (9in) deep will make shelves for marginal plants. As a reflective pool may be more effective with few or no marginal plants, the shelves need not go all the way around the edge.

5 Dig out the deeper zone of the pool to a finished depth of about 60cm (2ft). Dispose of this subsoil and do not use it in the garden.

6 Rake over the bottom to achieve a rough level and remove any sharp stones. Trim off exposed roots with secateurs. Smooth over the sides and marginal shelves, patting them to give a reasonably firm surface.

7 Line the hole with a sheet of underlay and trim off any excess around the edges.

8 Insert the flexible liner into the excavation, pleating the corners as much as possible before this becomes impossible with the weight of the water. Remember that the liner will be taken underneath the surrounding paving slabs and lipped vertically at the back of the slabs.

9 The liner will move about until some water is added, so half-fill the pool before laying the paving around the edge.

10 To prepare for the paving, skim off a thin layer of soil around the pool, 2.5cm (1in) deeper than the paving slabs. Remove the level pegs from around the pool. Spread a layer of soft sand where the slabs will be placed and extend the liner over the sand so the small lip is left sticking up. Prepare stiff ready-mixed mortar in a wheelbarrow and put five small dabs, one in the centre and one in each corner, where a slab will sit on the liner.

11 Lay a slab on the dabs of mortar, tapping it gently with the handle of a lump hammer until it is level. Check this with a spirit level. If the slab has a riven or uneven surface, use a straight-edge on the slab rather than the spirit level alone. Continue laying slabs, butting the sides close to each other and checking before the mortar sets that each slab is level in both directions and with its neighbours.

12 You are now left with the small flap of liner sticking out from under the edge of the slabs. If the paving is to be extended beyond one slab

around the pool nip the liner vertically between the next line of slabs and trim off the excess with a craft knife to the top of the slab. If you do not plan to extend the paved area beyond a single course, the lip of the liner must be wedged vertically against the outer edge of the slab by compressing soil, gravel or cobbles to hold it.

13 When the mortar has set completely the pool can be filled with water and planted.

Above A turf edge borders this reflective pool. The water reaches the underside of the turf in order to cut out distracting reflections.

Practicalities

Measuring the liner

Bringing the edge of the liner behind any hard paving or brick edge and creating a vertical lip behind the slabs means that the water level can reach the top of the surrounding edge. This technique increases the amount of flexible liner required, but is worth the extra expense. For this example, of a 2.4m (8ft) square pool with a maximum depth of 60cm (2ft) and surrounding paving slabs 60cm wide and about 5cm (2in) deep, the calculation is as follows: 2.4m (8ft) + 60cm (2ft) + 60cm (2ft) + 60cm (2ft) + 60cm (2ft) + 8cm (3in) + 8cm (3in). This gives a total size of 4.96m (16ft 6in) square.

FORMAL POOL

Among the simplest and quickest pools to install are small, formal pre-formed units. Although pre-formed liners are more expensive than flexible liners, the expense is justified for a small pool, especially when time and skill are limited. If possible, choose a top-of-the-range fibreglass pool, as these are stronger than the plastic types, have completely rigid sides and will be easier to keep level.

These small pools fit well into patio areas where they can be surrounded by paving slabs, which are very useful for concealing the rigid edges of the pre-formed liner. The most common shapes for formal pools are square, rectangular or circular in outline, and the pre-formed units eliminate all the folding of flexible liners in the corners or tight angles of small formal pools.

Tools & equipment

Wheelbarrow
Spade
Rake
Plasterer's trowel
Spirit level and straight-edge
Tamping tool, such as a cut-down broom handle
Extending metal tape measure

Materials

Pre-formed pool with a formal shape
Soft sand
Paving slabs, 60cm (2ft) square, to edge the pool
1–2 x 25kg bags of ready-mixed mortar
Aquatic plants
Aquatic planting compost
Planting baskets

1   Get help and turn the unit upside-down in its proposed position. Mark the outline with a line of sand around the perimeter of the unit.

2   Remove the pre-formed pool. Before you begin to dig the hole, measure the depth of the marginal shelf that has been built into the unit.

3   From just outside the marked outline begin digging out the topsoil to the same depth as the marginal shelf. Store this topsoil on a sheet of polythene nearby because it will be useful later for firming around the walls of the pool.

4   Once the depth of the shelf is reached, rake over the freshly dug surface to make a level tilth.

5   Get help again to lift the pool into the hole and press it down on the raked surface where it will make an

FORMAL POOL

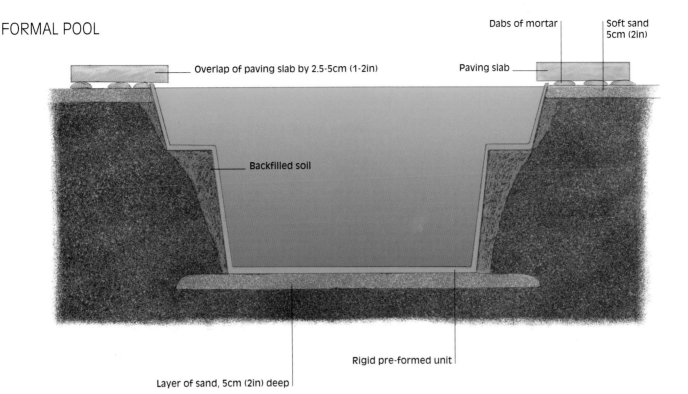

Dabs of mortar

Soft sand 5cm (2in)

Overlap of paving slab by 2.5-5cm (1-2in)

Paving slab

Backfilled soil

Rigid pre-formed unit

Layer of sand, 5cm (2in) deep

impression of the deeper zone. Lift the pool out again, and check that the imprint is clear before making a mark with sand around the outline. This will be a guide to the next area to be excavated.

6 From just outside the marked outline dig out the soil to the full depth of the pool, allowing an extra 5cm (2in) for a bed of sand on the bottom. An accurate measurement for the pool depth can be made by placing a straight-edge across the sides of the pool and measuring from the bottom of the timber edge to the floor of the pool with an extending metal tape measure.

7 Rake over the base of the hole and remove any stones from the bottom and sides. Spread a 5cm (2in) layer of soft sand over the bottom. Use a spirit level and straight-edge to check that the sand is as level as possible.

8 Get help and lower the pool gently into place. Check that the sides are level by placing the straight-edge over the opposite sides and holding the spirit level on top; do this in several directions. When you are sure that the pool is level, add about 10cm (4in) of water to the pool to help keep it stable.

9 Sift the excavated topsoil to remove all stones and sharp objects and use it to begin to fill the gap between the sides of the pool and the hole. Consolidate the backfilled soil by tamping or firming with a piece of wood, such as a cut-down broom handle. Backfill to correspond with the level of the water inside and check that this disturbance has not affected the level of the pool.

10 Repeat this process, adding about 15cm (6in) of water and a similar level of sifted soil on the outside, firming the soil thoroughly until the water reaches a depth of

about 5–8cm (2–3in) from the top edge of the pool.

11 Plant the submerged oxygenators as soon as possible in aquatic planting baskets on the pool bottom. If waterlilies and marginals are to be planted, these will also benefit the pool chemistry by being planted as soon as possible.

12 Edge the pool with a surround of 60cm (2ft) square paving slabs. Prepare a good base for the slabs by removing 5–8cm (2–3in) of the surrounding soil and replacing it with the same depth of soft sand. Prepare a stiff mix of ready-mixed mortar and lay dabs of mortar, one in each corner and one in the centre, in the proposed slab position. The slab should overlap the pool edge by 2.5–5cm (1–2in) and be level and stable. Make sure that each slab is level by tapping it down firmly with the handle of a lump hammer and checking it with a spirit level.

Opposite Turning the bricks round so that they are at 90 degrees to the water has given this pool a very strong, formal outline.

INFORMAL POOL

An informal pool can be constructed either by using a pre-formed shape or by creating a shape of your own using a flexible liner. The informal pool is more plant orientated than the formal pool, and is particularly suited to areas where any surrounding planting is also informal, naturalistic-looking and apparently unstructured.

Although there is greater freedom of variety in the outlines of informal pools, avoid shapes that are too fussy and have narrow promontories.

Because an informal pool is more likely to be sited further away from the house than a formal pool, the angle of the viewing point dictates that, if anything of the water surface is to be seen, a wider pool be built than is necessary for one seen from close quarters or from above. In the two weekends allowed for the construction, allocate as much time as possible to creating size, leaving much of the detail of the surroundings to be fine tuned later on. Make the pond as large as time and space permit, this not only helps in managing the water but also allows greater variety in the plant choice.

Materials

Pegs, about 2.5cm (1in) in
   diameter and 23cm (9in) long
Flexible liner
Underlay
4–5 x 25kg bags of rounded
   washed cobbles
2–3 x 25kg bags of soft sand
3–4 paving slabs, at least 60cm
   (24in) across
Plants
Aquatic planting baskets
Aquatic compost

Tools & equipment

Spade
Rake
Wheelbarrow
Hosepipe or string
Spirit level and straight-edge
Secateurs
Scissors
Lump hammer
Edging iron if installing the pool
   into an existing lawn
Expanding metal tape measure
Bricks or heavy stones
Pegs

1 Mark out the pool outline with string or hosepipe and view it from several angles before marking the outline in sand. The shape will look quite different from a distance, and using a hosepipe or string allows you to make changes very easily during this important stage.

2 When you are satisfied with the shape, insert pegs just outside the outline of the pool at intervals of about 1m (3ft). This is to identify any variations in level around the pool so that the necessary adjustments can be made around the outline before the pool is installed.

3 Decide which peg is going to be used to identify the finished water level and knock this in with a lump hammer so that the top of the peg represents the required point.

4 Knock in the other pegs so that their tops are all at the same height as the first peg. Use a spirit level and straight-edge to check this. When all the pegs are knocked in level it will be clear whether any soil will have to be added or removed before excavations begin.

5 Begin digging out at a slight angle from vertical around the sides to a depth of 23cm (9in) across the pool. If part of the pool edge is to form a beach, leave this area for grading later.

6 Roughly rake the surface of the freshly dug soil and then mark an outline in sand for the deeper area of the pool. This can allow for the shallow marginal shelf all the way round the pool or for part of the edge only.

7 Dig out the deeper part to a further 38cm (15in) so that the bottom of the pool is 60cm (2ft) deep. The soil excavated in this deeper zone is not suitable for growing plants, and unless major alterations to levels in other parts of the garden are envisaged, this subsoil should be disposed of.

8 Rake over the pool bottom and pat down the sides. Remove any stones and trim off any exposed roots with secateurs.

2

Two Weekend Projects

Right A lovely combination of aquatics and moisture-loving plants shows how even a small pool can bring lushness and varied form to garden planting.

9 Insert the underlay over the whole excavation, holding down the sides with stones until the liner is in position.

10 Insert the liner. Check beforehand how it has been folded so that unrolling will be more straightforward. You will find this process easier if someone can help you, and there will be less disturbance to the underlay if a second pair of hands can hold one side of the liner.

11 Secure the liner temporarily around the edge of the pool with bricks or stones so that the sides do not get blown into the pool.

12 As long as you are wearing soft-soled shoes, it is safe to stand inside the pool on the liner so that you can push it into the pool outline and make pleats in any tight curves.

13 Add water from a hosepipe to the level of the deeper zone. You can now stand on any marginal shelves to plant submerged oxygenating plants and deep-water plants, such as waterlilies. These should be introduced into the pool in aquatic planting baskets as described on pages 136–7.

14 You can now fill to within 5–8cm (2–3in) of the final level so that the marginal plants can be placed in containers around the marginal shelves.

15 The water level will now show if the edge is level. Make any final adjustments before trimming the liner and making an edge. The edge for an informal pool can be made with several materials or all in one style; see pages 108–9 for edging an informal pool. Once the edging is chosen and completed, fill the pool to the finished level.

Practicalities

Edging the pool

To get easier access to the pool, finish part of the edge with a more stable material such as two or three paving slabs. Remove 5–8cm (2–3in) of the soil just beyond the liner on the area where the slabs will be positioned. Spread a level layer of sand, 5–8cm (2–3in) deep, over this area before positioning the slabs. Their edges should overlap the water by 2.5cm (1in) and they must sit absolutely level on top of the sand. Large slabs 60cm (2ft) or more square will be stable enough near an informal pool without a mortar foundation, but smaller slabs will require dabs of mortar under them.

INFORMAL POOL

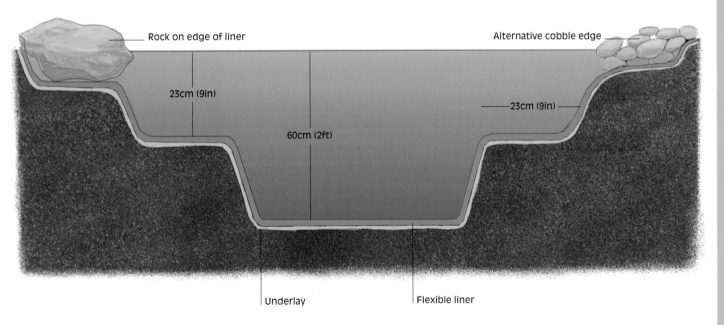

Rock on edge of liner

Alternative cobble edge

23cm (9in)

23cm (9in)

60cm (2ft)

Underlay

Flexible liner

INFORMAL BOG AREA

Strictly, a bog is an area of soil that is often waterlogged. In the ornamental water garden the term more often refers to an area of moist but not waterlogged soil, which is constructed separately from, but often adjacent to, the main pool. The addition of a bog area to an informal pool will extend the range of plants that you can grow and can bridge the gap between a pond and, for example, a wildlife meadow.

In water garden catalogues, plants for bog gardens are often listed as 'moisture-lovers' because the plants listed will tolerate a degree of waterlogging but prefer more oxygen around the roots than the true 'bog plant', which would be listed as a marginal aquatic.

In a small garden an informal bog area could be created on its own without a pool, simply as a means of growing some of the vast range of plants that thrive in these conditions. A bog area can also be created next to an informal pool so that it appears to be an extension of the pool, but an advantage of creating the bog independently is that it makes no demands on the water in the pool, which could drop in level in dry periods. The bog garden is watered independently with a semi-automatic system and a small amount of slow drainage is provided to allow oxygen to the roots of the plants. The bog need not take up a large area, but its impact on an informal water feature is considerable and it is best regarded as a separate project, to be undertaken after the construction of an informal pool.

Tools & equipment

Spade
Garden fork
Knife or scissors
Dowelling or wine bottle cork
Bradawl or small drill

Materials

Heavy-duty polythene
Pea shingle
Length of non-kinkable or
     reinforced garden hosepipe
Organic soil enriching compost
Garden hosepipe connector
Moisture-loving plants

INFORMAL BOG GARDEN

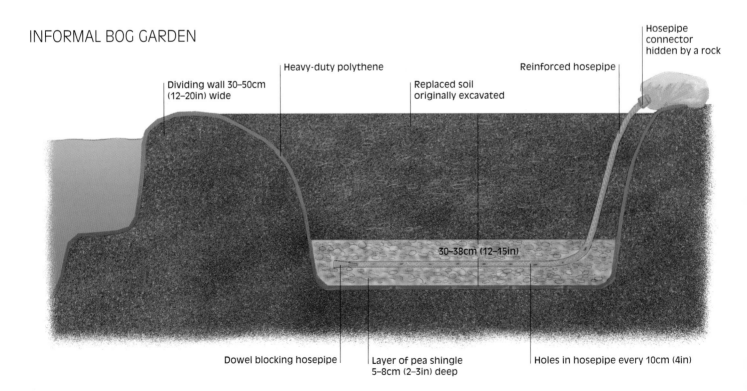

Dividing wall 30–50cm (12–20in) wide

Heavy-duty polythene

Replaced soil originally excavated

Reinforced hosepipe

Hosepipe connector hidden by a rock

30–38cm (12–15in)

Dowel blocking hosepipe

Layer of pea shingle 5–8cm (2–3in) deep

Holes in hosepipe every 10cm (4in)

1 Mark out the site, which can either be next to an existing pool or in an area on its own, perhaps edging a wildflower meadow or area of rough grass left long so that the foliage of spring bulbs can die down. If it is next to a pool, leave 30–50cm (12–20in) between the bog and the pool so that digging for the bog does not make the liner bulge and the water overflow.

2 Dig out the soil to a depth of 30–38cm (12–15in). Place the excavated soil on a spare piece of heavy-duty polythene.

3 Measure the hole, including the height of the walls, and insert a sheet of heavy-duty polythene into the hole so that a slight surplus sticks up over the sides all round.

4 Make small slits in the bottom of the polythene or pierce it with a fork. Make the holes few and far between; if there are too many, the bog will drain too quickly. One small slit, 8cm (3in) long, every 1m (3ft) will be adequate. All that is required is for the soil to have time to retain moisture for a while before it seeps away slowly.

5 Cover the bottom of the polythene with 5–8cm (2–3in) of rounded pea shingle or river-washed gravel that is not sharp. If you use sharp gravel the liner may be pierced and cause the bog to drain too quickly.

6 Introduce a length of strong or reinforced (non-kinkable) 13mm (½in) hosepipe into the pea shingle. It should be long enough to lie along the bottom of the bog then turn up the side and jut out from the surface by 5–8cm (2–3in). Seal the end of the pipe with a length of dowelling, shaved to the diameter of the pipe. Alternatively,

cut a wine cork to size and use it to stop the end of the hosepipe. It is not necessary for the sealed end to be entirely waterproof; the function of this rough and ready seal is simply to stop the rush of water out of the end of the pipe. Use a bradawl or fine drill to pierce the hosepipe with small holes every 10cm (4in) along its length; these holes will let the water seep out. Bury the hose in pea shingle to stop the holes being clogged up with soil.

7 Fit a female garden hose connector to the end of the hosepipe protruding above ground. This will allow it to be connected to the garden hose whenever the bog requires topping up with water in dry spells. This could be as often as every week in hot weather. When you are topping up, leave the hose connected until you can see water seeping from the soil surface, causing minimal consolidation of

the soil but making sure that the soil is thoroughly soaked.

8 Return the excavated soil to the hole. If the soil is poor in quality, now is a good time to add plenty of organic matter, which will help it to retain moisture. If the soil is of really poor quality, simply refill the hole with a good, humus-rich loam or compost and dispose of the poor soil.

9 Roughly level off the soil in the bog area and cut off any liner that is protruding around the edges. The short length of hosepipe and connector can be protected in a polythene bag and hidden by a stone.

10 Planting can now begin. The moisture-loving plants should be watered in from above after planting, but then connect the hosepipe to the connector in the bed and allow the water to soak the soil thoroughly.

Above A typical bog garden mix in late spring dominated by candelabra primulas and *Trollius*.

RAISED POOL

The easiest type of raised pool to make is one that uses a rigid pre-formed liner, which sits on the ground and is surrounded by a decorative wall that disguises the sides of the pool and provides support for its rigid sides. Construction is made much easier if the pre-formed liner is made of fibreglass because the sides are stronger and it is much easier to create a level rim than with the semi-rigid plastic types.

Right Railway sleepers make excellent surrounds for raised pools, especially as they are substantial enough to sit on.

A raised pool is an excellent focal point on a patio or in a courtyard garden. Choose a site that is as level as possible, particularly if the base is of concrete or paving, where it would be difficult to make major alterations to the level.

1   Before you order the railway sleepers, choose the size and shape of pre-formed pool that will occupy the space inside the sleepers. Both formal and informal shapes of rigid pool can be used, because the gaps between the rigid pool sides and the sleepers can be landscaped with a variety of materials, including, gravel, rocks and plants.

2   Mark out the shape of the rigid pool on the proposed site. Draw around this the surrounding box shape so that you can calculate the number of sleepers that will be required. If you are awaiting delivery of the rigid pool, make a small plan on graph paper to plan the dimensions of the scheme.

3   The sleepers are used to make a frame, just under 2.4m (8ft) square. The project assumes that the sleepers are 20cm (8in) deep, so that walls of three sleepers will contain a rigid pool 45cm (18in) deep. This gives space for a layer of soft sand under the rigid pool without having to excavate a base and makes it easier if you are building on a concrete or paved base.

4   Mark out the base square for the sleepers and place a 5–8cm (2–3in) layer of pea shingle or soft sand along the line that will be occupied by the timbers. This material will help you to make any alterations of angle that may be necessary in order to level the timbers, as well

Tools & equipment

Spade
Rake
Spirit level and straight-edge
Small wooden wedges
Tamping tool, such as a cut-down
    broom handle
Screwdriver
Hammer

Materials

Rigid pre-formed pool
Railway sleepers
Soft sand or pea shingle
Right-angle brackets and screws
Large galvanized nails
Heavy-duty polythene
Sifted topsoil or bags of multi-
    purpose compost
Alpine and aquatic plants
Small rocks
Alpine grit

RAISED POOL

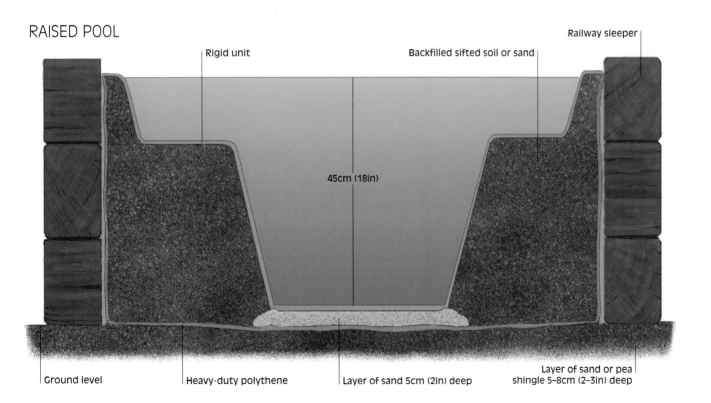

Rigid unit

Backfilled sifted soil or sand

Railway sleeper

45cm (18in)

Ground level

Heavy-duty polythene

Layer of sand 5cm (2in) deep

Layer of sand or pea shingle 5–8cm (2–3in) deep

Below Partially
raised pools make
ideal centrepieces
for a formal garden,
especially if a
fountain is
introduced.

as providing useful drainage
directly under them. Make sure
that the sand or pea shingle base
for the sleepers is absolutely level
by checking in all directions with a
spirit level on a straight-edge.
Make any slight adjustments to the
layer of sand or shingle.

5 Get help with placing the first
course of sleepers into place.
Check that the tops are as level as
possible because there may be
some slight discrepancies in their
thickness.

6 When you are satisfied with the
level of the first layer, lift the
second layer into place, bonding
the position so that the ends are
not in line with the layer below.
Check the levels again. Major
discrepancies can be overcome by
the use of thin wedges of wood to
pack the lower ends.

7 Put the final layer in position,
taking particular care to ensure
that the tops are level and that you
are using the best surfaces of the
sleepers.

8 When the framework is in place,
make it more stable by screwing
right-angle brackets into the
corners so that two sleepers are
joined by a bracket at every corner.
Knocking in long galvanized nails at
an angle from one sleeper to the
one underneath will also increase
the rigidity.

9 Line the inside of the framework
of the sleepers with a sheet of
heavy-duty polythene. This will
prevent the soil that is packed
between the rigid pool and the
sleeper being forced out of any
gaps between the sleepers and
help to increase the rigidity and
strength of the frame.

10 Spread a layer of soft sand, about
5cm (2in) deep, over the inside
base and rake this as level as
possible.

11 You will need help in lifting the
rigid pool into the frame and
position it so that there is an
adequate gap all the way round,
which will be filled with soil or
sand. Check that the sides of the
rigid pool are level with a spirit
level on a straight-edge that is
long enough to rest on the
opposite sides. Check the level
in all directions.

12 When you are entirely satisfied that
the pool is level, pour about 10cm
(4in) of water into the pool to
stabilize it and then begin to pack
and consolidate sifted soil or sand
around the sides. Check the level
when the height of the soil or sand
is equal to the height of water in
the pool.

13 Continue to add water and keep
consolidating the soil between
the pool and the sleepers. The
rounded end of a cut-down
broom handle is useful for helping

to get the soil thoroughly firmed. Keep checking the level of the pool in case the soil and increasing weight of water affect its position.

14 When the packed soil reaches the rim of the pool, the water plants can be planted and the surround can be landscaped with small flat rocks and alpine plants. A top-dressing of coarse grit or alpine grit makes an attractive finish to the surround.

Above This small raised pool has been given a beautiful surround with tiles that reflect warm, sunny climates.

raised pool **85**

SEMI-RAISED POOL WITH LOG ROLL SURROUND

A semi-raised pool has two advantages over one that is totally above ground. First, the water in the deeper zone will be frozen only in prolonged and severe winter weather. Second, because the water pressure on the sides of the pool is reduced as only the top 23–30cm (9–12in) of it is above the ground, you can use a less expensive semi-rigid pool and less substantial, more decorative surrounds.

A semi-raised pool is suitable for a patio or paved area only if you can remove the hard surfacing to excavate a hole for the deep zone of the pool. Semi-raised pools are useful on sloping sites, where one side of the pool may be at ground level and the other just above ground level, which makes installation on such sites much easier than with a flexible liner or a totally raised pool.

Right Log roll is an adaptable form of edging that lends itself to almost any shape of pool.

Tools & equipment

Rake
Spade
Spirit level and straight-edge
Tamping tool, such as a cut-down
   broom handle
Lump hammer
Wirecutters

Materials

Rigid pool
Soft sand
Pointed timber stakes 45 x 4cm
   (18 x 1½in)
Log roll 23cm (9in) high
Galvanized nails 5cm (2in) long
Galvanized wire to join lengths of
   log roll if required
Alpine and aquatic plants
Small rocks
Alpine grit

1 Rake the proposed site to clear away stones and debris so that the base of the deeper zone of the rigid unit will make an impression on the freshly raked surface. If the rigid unit is bulky, get some help with carefully placing the unit in position. Press it down by pushing hard on the inside of the deeper zone. If all sides are accessible, a long stick can be used to mark the edge of the base to give extra clarity to the imprint.

2 Put the pool on one side and dig out a hole 5cm (2in) deeper than the deep zone of the pool. Start digging 5cm (2in) outside the outline left by the imprint and shape the sides of the hole so that they are slightly sloping.

3 Rake the bottom of the hole level and spread an even layer of sand, 5cm (2in) deep, over the area.

4 Gently lift the rigid pool back into the hole and check that the sides are level by placing a straight-edge with a spirit level on top across the sides. Make any necessary adjustments to the level by lifting the pool out and adding or removing sand.

5 Pour about 10cm (4in) of water into the pool to give it some stability and begin to backfill around the sides with sifted soil or sand. Check again that the sides are still level.

6 Continue adding water and backfilling so that the levels on each side of the pool remain the same. When the area around the deep zone has been completely backfilled and the water in the pool is to a depth of about 23cm (9in), knock in the stakes to support the log roll surround, positioning them in a line that is parallel to the perimeter of the pool and that allows sufficient room for planting and landscaping between the pool and the log roll surround. The

stakes should be placed at intervals of about 1m (3ft), and they should be driven into the ground so that the tops of the stakes are at the same height as the lip edge of the rigid pool

7 Unroll the sections of log roll and position them around the pool. The rolls are usually sold in lengths of 1m (3ft), so that if more than one section is needed it can be joined to another by wire. If there is too much at the end of a roll, use wirecutters to shorten the section. The timbers can be partially buried if they are higher at any point than the lip of the pool.

8 Nail the log roll at top and bottom to the stakes.

9 Backfill the area between the upper zone of the pool and the

log rolls with sifted soil. Then consolidate the soil firmly with a tamping tool until it is level with the top of the pool.

10 Plant the aquatics and marginal plants in the pool before landscaping the sides with small rocks and alpines.

SEMI-RAISED POOL

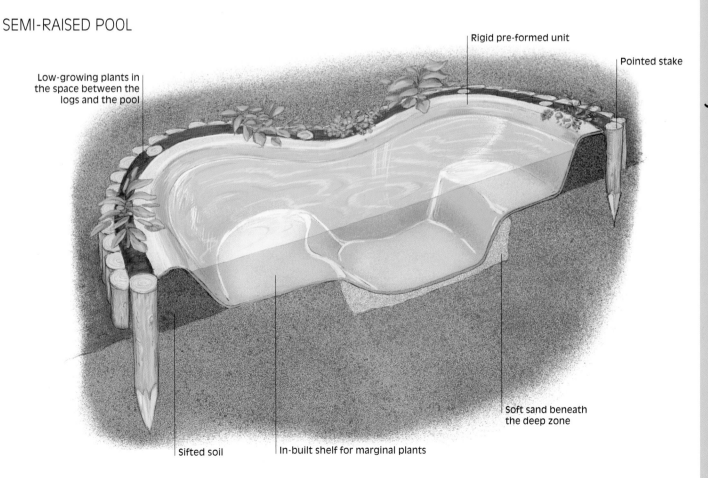

Low-growing plants in the space between the logs and the pool

Rigid pre-formed unit

Pointed stake

Sifted soil

In-built shelf for marginal plants

Soft sand beneath the deep zone

ROCK AND PEBBLE POOL

The attraction of a pebble pool is that it is shallow, reasonably safe for gardens where children are likely to play and will fit into a small, sunny niche. The shallowness and small size are, however, the major causes of difficulties in maintaining water clarity. As no planting is envisaged to keep the water clear it will need a well-hidden clarification system.

The pool is shallow but you should allow an area at least 1.2m (4ft) across together with space for the 'bridge' of railway sleepers, under which the pump and water clarifier will be hidden. This type of pool would suit an informal area of the garden, where it can be planted with graceful ferns and hostas.

Tools & equipment

Spade

Rake

Wheelbarrow

Screwdriver

Hacksaw

Scissors

Small drill or bradawl

Spirit level and straight-edge

Materials

Flexible liner and underlay

Underwater filter kit or filter
    medium (such as Lytag) and
    flexible reinforced pipe, 13mm
    (½in) in diameter and 2m (6ft) long

Cork or wooden dowelling

Submersible pump

Ultraviolet clarifier

Flexible pipe long enough to
    be cut into two lengths (see
    step 6)

Hose clips

Magnet limescale attachment

Railway sleepers

Cobbles, rocks and boulders

1 Mark out the site. An informal shape – an ovoid, oval or near circle – would be appropriate, but do not make it too small or it will be difficult to install an effective filtration system. The sides should have shallow shelves 10–15cm (4–6in deep), and the flat bottom should be at least 45cm (18in) deep and 1–1.2m (3–4ft) in diameter.

2 Drape underlay into the hole, then insert the flexible liner and push it into place. Secure the sides of the liner temporarily with cobbles, leaving ample overlap in the liner so that you can make adjustments when the water is added.

3 The pool uses an underwater filtration system. You can either buy a proprietary kit or make your own. If you make your own, coil a flexible plastic pipe on the pool bottom. Before coiling the pipe, make numerous small holes in it, about 2.5cm (1in) apart, and seal one end of the pipe with a bung made from cork or wooden dowelling shaved to size. The other end of the pipe will be attached to the intake of a submersible pump.

4 Bury the coiled pipe in a 10cm (4in) layer of a porous filter medium, such as Lytag (lightweight, baked clay granules, which are a waste product of the electricity industry).

5 The pump and an ultraviolet clarifier will need to be disguised, and an easy way to do this is to create a simple bridge over the pool with a single railway sleeper or two railway sleepers side by side. The pump will be almost hidden in the water under the bridge, and the ultraviolet clarifier can be fitted above the water level by screwing it to the underside of the sleeper. Choose a point of the pool that is no wider than 2m (6ft) across and

ROCK AND PEBBLE POOL

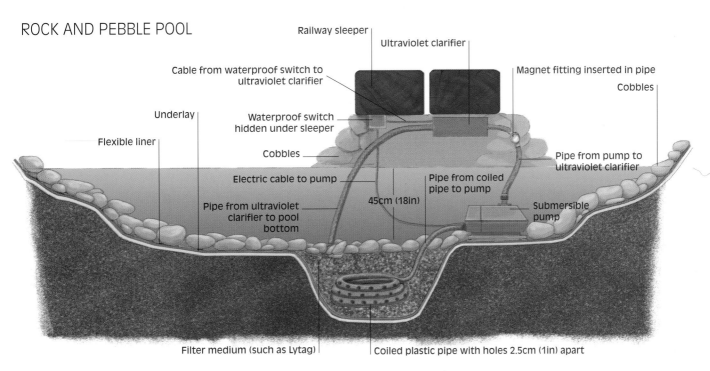

Railway sleeper
Ultraviolet clarifier
Cable from waterproof switch to ultraviolet clarifier
Magnet fitting inserted in pipe
Cobbles
Underlay
Waterproof switch hidden under sleeper
Flexible liner
Cobbles
Pipe from pump to ultraviolet clarifier
Electric cable to pump
Pipe from coiled pipe to pump
Pipe from ultraviolet clarifier to pool bottom
45cm (18in)
Submersible pump
Filter medium (such as Lytag)
Coiled plastic pipe with holes 2.5cm (1in) apart

lay the sleeper across it. This arrangement means that the ends of the sleeper will be supported on the cobble surround. Use a spirit level to check that the sleeper is level. The ends can be partially buried in the cobble surround, and small cobbles can be used to adjust the height of either end.

6   A length of flexible delivery pipe from the pump is now connected to the intake of the ultraviolet clarifier and secured to it with a hose clip. Another length of flexible pipe is taken from the outlet of the ultraviolet clarifier back into the pool and lodged between some cobbles on top of the filter medium. This creates an internal circulation system around the pool.

7   As a further aid against the development of blanketweed use a proprietary magnet attachment, which is inserted into the flexible pipe by cutting the pipe, inserting the magnet fitting, then rejoining

both sides of the magnet fitting with hose clips. This fitting works in a similar way to the domestic attachments that are sold for reducing limescale in waterpipes, by reducing the alkaline conditions in which blanketweed thrives.

8   Spread round washed cobbles over the filter medium on the pool bottom and over the sloping sides of the pool until they cover the edges of the liner. When the pool is filled, it becomes a relatively simple matter to adjust the edges of the liner, using the waterline as the guide. The edge of the liner is kept above the finished waterline, and the cobbles are used to hide its edge.

9   To provide variety to the cobbles, add some larger rounded boulders at random around the pool, some partially submerged and some on the surround. If the style of the garden is sympathetic to rocks, pieces of rock can be used in the pool surround.

Practicalities

Keeping the water clear

The project requires a pump, a filter and an ultraviolet clarifier, all of which can be unsightly (the time needed for introducing a cable into the garden has not been taken into account). This scheme outlines one of several available methods for disguising these essentials and for installing a chemical-free water-purification system. Even with clear water, however, algae will build up on the surface of the pebbles and will have to be cleaned from time to time. Blanketweed, which thrives in clear water, can be another menace in pools like this. If you are prepared to remove any early growth by hand and not use mains water to top up the pool, a clear pebble pool can be achieved.

Opposite
An idyllic and reasonably safe shallow pebble pool where the bridge also disguises a submersible pump and clarifier.

CASCADING STREAM WITH PRE-FORMED UNITS

This is one of the most usual styles of small stream for a small garden because it uses the soil removed during the building of a pool to make a small mound to create waterfalls. The project assumes that there is an existing pool, but if no such pool exists, a reservoir makes a good alternative. Using pre-formed units for the cascade means that the watercourse can be built quickly, with few building skills needed.

Assuming that three units, each about 1m (3ft) long and 30cm (12in) wide, are used, you will also need a separate rock pool, about 1m (3ft) across, to act as the header pool at the top of the watercourse. This combination would mean that an ideal site would need a minimum diameter of 5m (15ft) and a height of no more than 1m (3ft) to create a natural-looking effect in an otherwise flat garden. The project assumes that there is an existing pool for the stream to spill into.

Tools & equipment

Pegs
String or sand
Tape measure
Spade
Trowel
Spirit level and straight-edge
Watering can

Materials

Pre-formed stream units
Pre-formed rock pool to act as a
    header pool
Soft sand
Submersible pump
Length of corrugated plastic pipe
    to act as the delivery pipe
    from the pump to the origin
    of the stream; use a 2.5cm
    (1in) diameter pipe if the
    length required is greater
    than 1m (3ft)
Rocks and stones
Low-growing plants

Right A good supply of flat rocks and coordinated carpeting plants hides the materials used to make this delightful stream.

1 Mark out a route for the stream with string or sand. As the length of each stream unit is known, mark where they will overlap. Natural streams seldom travel in a straight line down a rocky watercourse, so vary the direction of each unit at the junction points.

2 Working from the bottom, dig out a shallow trench, 2.5–5cm (1–2in) deeper than the stream unit and sloping slightly to the mound.

3 Line the trench with a covering of soft sand 2.5–5cm (1–2in) deep.

4 Bed the first unit on the sand with the lower end overlapping the pool by 5–8cm (2–3in). Check the level by pouring some water in to each unit to see if a small amount of water remains. If water stays in the

stream when the pump is turned off, it will have a more natural and permanent look and also provide small bathing areas for birds.

5 Repeat the process with the next two sections, making sure that the lip at the bottom end of each unit overlaps the one below it.

6 The header pool, which is deeper than the stream units, will be positioned at the top end of the stream. Dig a hole slightly deeper and wider than the pool and line it with a layer of sand 5cm (2in) deep. Make sure that this is level by laying a spirit level across the sides in all directions. Arrange the pool so that the integral pouring lip flows into the stream unit below.

7 When all the units are in place, firm the soil around the edges of the stream sections and header pool.

8 Insert a submersible pump in the base pool close to the outlet of the waterfall. Connect a corrugated plastic pipe to the delivery outlet of the pump and bury this in a shallow trench 60–90cm (2–3ft) away from the stream units so it is not disturbed. The end of the pipe is placed just over the top edge of the header pool and disguised with small rocks. Keep the end of the delivery pipe above the water level in the header pool to prevent the water siphoning back to the base pool through the pipe.

9 Connect the pump to a waterproof switch or socket near the pool. Turn on the pump and make any adjustments to the amount of water flowing through the stream units by altering the flow adjuster on the pump. To make this adjustment easier and save having to place your hand in the water, fit a small flow regulator to the delivery pipe just before it enters the header pool.

10 Place a few strategic rocks and stones along the edge of the stream, and plant low-growing and creeping species near the stream edge so that they will eventually disguise the hard rim of the units.

CASCADING STREAM WITH PRE-FORMED UNITS

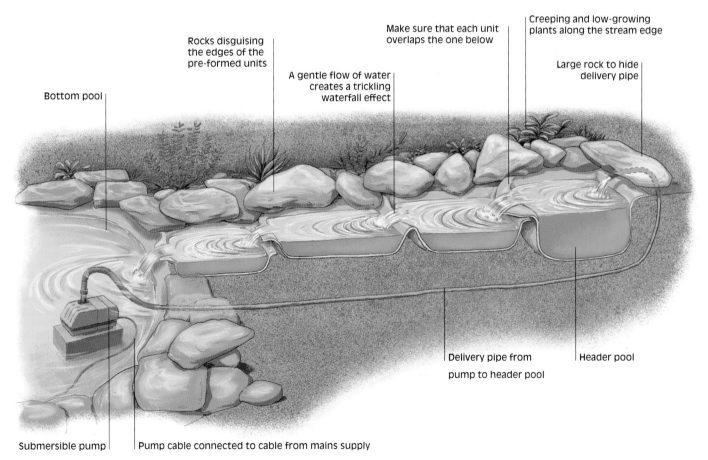

Rocks disguising the edges of the pre-formed units

Make sure that each unit overlaps the one below

Creeping and low-growing plants along the stream edge

A gentle flow of water creates a trickling waterfall effect

Large rock to hide delivery pipe

Bottom pool

Delivery pipe from pump to header pool

Header pool

Submersible pump

Pump cable connected to cable from mains supply

MEANDERING STREAM WITH A FLEXIBLE LINER

This meandering stream requires no more than a few centimetres of fall along its length, and the source can be made from a few rocks, to create a slight elevation and disguise the end of the delivery pipe. If you do not already have a pool or do not envisage creating one, a reservoir for the stream to spill into can be made in the same way as for the cobble fountain on pages 54–5, although it may need to be larger.

This type of stream will look more natural if there is lush planting along parts of the sides and bottom of the stream. It should vary in direction and width, copying nature by having wider, shallow areas on any curves and narrower, straighter sections where there is an appreciable slope. A selection of flat rocks with rounded tops, smooth boulders and river-washed cobbles will be useful for disguising any awkward, protruding edges of the liner.

Tools & equipment

Hosepipe or string
Spirit level and straight-edge
Pegs and hammer
Half-moon edging tool
Rake
Wheelbarrow
Scissors

Materials

Heavy-duty polythene
Flexible liner
Underlay
Submersible pump
Corrugated plastic pipe
Rocks and pebbles
Pea shingle
Flat piece of rock (spillstone)
1 x 25kg bag of ready-mixed
   mortar
Flow-regulating valve (optional)
Oxygenating and marginal plants

1 Mark out the route of the stream with a hosepipe or string and look at the route critically from the main viewpoints, including the most frequented windows in the house. Mark the width as well as the direction of the stream, which should vary from 30–38cm (12–15in) to 1m (3ft) in parts. Check that the base of the stream will be almost level and that any slight slope is towards the base pool. Knock in pegs along the course of the route and check the level with a spirit level and straight-edge.

2 One of the most effective sites for the stream will be if it is cut into the lawn, so remove the turf by cutting the marked outline with a half-moon edging tool. Cut lines across the inside of the outline every 30cm (12in).

3 Use a spade to skim off sections of turf 5cm (2in) deep and store the turves upside-down somewhere out of sight. The turves will rot down to valuable loam in a few months.

4 The outline of the stream will now be clearly visible in the lawn. Make any adjustments needed to improve its shape.

5 Place a sheet of heavy-duty polythene next to the stream and begin digging out, placing the soil from the excavation on the polythene because it will be needed later. Where there are wide sections of the stream, excavate to create shallow sides, 15–23cm (6–9in) wide and 10–15cm (4–6in) deep, with a deeper section in the centre, 23–30cm (9–12in) deep. Narrow sections of the stream are simply dug out to the whole profile to a depth of 23–30cm (9–12in). The sides of the stream and any shelves should be cut out absolutely vertically and the base should be flat, not saucer-shaped, to prevent the top-dressing of soil slumping into the deeper area after the liner has been installed.

6 Create a shallow, flat-topped ridge in the soil just before the fall into the reservoir or base pool. Make the top of the ridge low enough to allow a thin, flat stone, such as a thin piece of slate, the spillstone, to sit on the top so that the stone is lower than the sides of the stream. This ridge will prevent all the water from draining from the stream when the pump is turned off.

7 Remove any stones, sharp objects and roots, then rake the base and any shelves to create a smooth, flat surface.

8 Drape underlay along the complete length of the stream, trimming off the excess overlap along the sides once it is in place.

Left Shallow rock and cobble streams allow infinite scope for creative design.

MEANDERING STREAM WITH A FLEXIBLE LINER

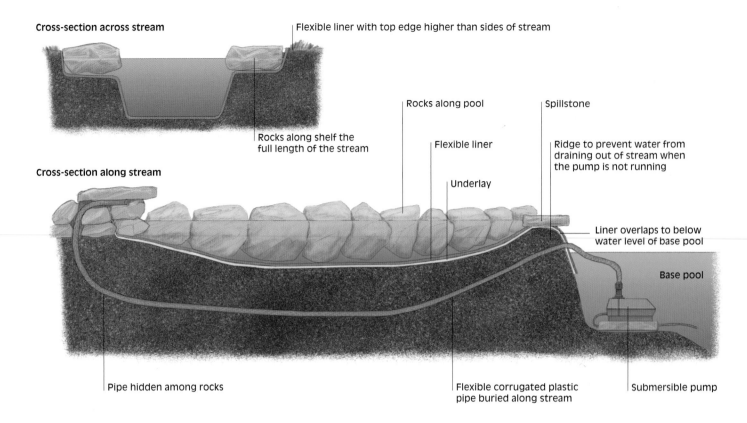

Cross-section across stream

Flexible liner with top edge higher than sides of stream

Rocks along shelf the full length of the stream

Rocks along pool

Flexible liner

Underlay

Spillstone

Ridge to prevent water from draining out of stream when the pump is not running

Cross-section along stream

Liner overlaps to below water level of base pool

Base pool

Pipe hidden among rocks

Flexible corrugated plastic pipe buried along stream

Submersible pump

9 Install the liner, leaving any overlap sticking out for the moment in case any adjustments are necessary later. Make sure that the exit point of the stream overlaps into the base pool or reservoir and is lower than the sides along the complete length of the stream. To allow water to remain in the stream when the pump is turned off, create a lip to hold the water back at the exit point. The top of the lip will be folded behind the spillstone at the same level as the top surface of the stone, which must be lower than the top of the stream sides.

10 To save making another trench in the lawn, tuck the delivery pipe of corrugated plastic pipe just under the side of the liner along the length of the stream, burying it sufficiently so that it does not protrude under the liner. Leave enough pipe at the reservoir end to attach to the pump in the reservoir and enough overlap at the stream source so that it can be turned around and hidden under some rocks just above the finished water level.

11 So that you have greater control over the flow rate down the stream, if you wish you can fit a flow-regulating valve into the top of the delivery pipe and hide it under a rock at the stream source.

12 Connect the pipe to a submersible pump in the reservoir or base pool.

13 Put the excavated soil on top of the liner. You will not need all of the soil, just enough to create a saucer-shaped depression in a layer 10–15cm (4–6in) thick and to make sure that the liner is completely covered.

14 Place the spillstone at the end of the stream on a base of stiff mortar, checking it is level and the top of the stone is lower than the stream sides. The mortar must dry and set before the water is pumped down the stream, so aim to have this stone in place before the end of the first weekend.

15 Arrange a small cluster of rocks on the liner at the stream source to allow the delivery pipe to be hidden as the water is pumped.

16 Cover the layer of soil in the stream with pea shingle and cobbles. Add some water and turn on the pump. Start the pump at the lowest flow rate until the stream is fully charged with water, then the rate can be gradually increased. This prevents any erosion of the fresh soil until it becomes saturated and settles.

17 Once the water is spilling into the pool or reservoir over the top of the spillstone, check that there are no areas down the sides of the stream where water may be overflowing. If it is necessary, simply raise the level of the spare overlap liner at the sides to correct any overflows.

18 When you are happy that the stream is flowing satisfactorily, the overlapping liner along the sides of the stream can be trimmed and folded out of sight under the surrounding turf. Flat-topped stones can be used to disguise any overlap that is too large to tuck under the turf.

19 Plant shallow-water marginals and oxygenators into the bottom and along the sides of the stream.

Above The water in this series of long shallow pools overflows from one to another.

The following two projects are a little more complex in construction and need additional time for the mortar to harden completely before the next stages can be undertaken. They are water features for completely different styles of garden: one informal and the other formal.

THREE WEEKEND PROJECTS

ROCKY STREAM AND WATERFALL

This project involves choosing suitable rocks to use along the stream sides and as waterfall stones. If you are planning to work single-handed, make sure that the rocks are not so heavy that you cannot handle them easily. In three weekends you should be able to build a feature that incorporates a base waterfall, a length of stream and a header pool spilling into the stream over a waterfall.

This type of water feature is often created to make use of the soil that has been excavated from a pool or to form a stream on a sloping site. It is generally more effective if the pool makes use of the same type of rock around the edges as the stream so that the two features will look integrated. The project assumes that there is already an existing pool in your garden for the stream to spill into.

Tools & equipment	Materials
Pegs, canes and string for initial marking out	Submersible pump
Spade	Length of flexible corrugated plastic hose
Secateurs	Flexible liner
Trowel	Underlay
Mortaring trowel	Rocks
Spirit level and straight-edge	Bags of ready-mixed mortar
Wheelbarrow	Pebbles and cobbles
Watering can	Marginal plants

Right The mainly light-coloured planting is a perfect complement to the dark water.

Opposite Scrambling *Alchemilla mollis* (Lady's mantle) is an excellent choice for edging a waterfall.

1 Mark out the route of the stream with canes, pegs and string. If there is enough room for a stream that can vary in width, it will look more interesting and natural if there are slight variations in its course so that it is not too straight. Mark the position of the proposed waterfall from the header pool so that a step can be made later when you are digging out the soil.

2 Starting at the edge of the existing pool, dig out a trench with a slight slope away from the bottom pool to the width required. The depth should be about 15cm (6in). Streams deeper than this will need larger rocks to form the edge, and these could be too heavy to handle easily on your own. The width of the stream must allow for the rocks edging the water to sit on the liner, and if an area of wet soil is required for marginal and

Below Go and look at real streams to get inspiration on how to create something that looks natural and coherent.

moisture-loving plants behind the rocks, the area excavated will need to be at least 60cm (2ft) wide. An excavation 60cm (2ft) wide will be sufficient for a stream with a water width of 15–20cm (6–8in), leaving adequate room for rocks and soil at the sides. You will have no difficulty in obtaining liners for almost any width of stream, but the wider the stream, the greater the size of pump that will be required to give an adequate rate of flow.

3 Make a vertical step where you require the header pool at the end of the trench and dig out the hole for a small pool that will be higher than the level of the stream. This pool can be any size you wish, but it should be deep enough to grow marginal and oxygenating plants. These plants will help to keep the pool clear, as the water may remain still if the pump is turned off for long periods. If the header pool is more than 30cm (12in) deep, make a marginal shelf 15cm (6in) deep around the sides to allow the rocks to sit on the shelf, thereby avoiding the need to use very large rocks to form the edge.

4 Rake the whole area to remove stones and sharp objects. Trim any exposed roots with secateurs.

5 Drape underlay into the whole excavation. Keep the underlay well away from the water level in the base pool because it makes a very efficient wick and will suck quite large quantities of water out of the pool.

6 Partly unroll the liner, draping the unrolled end over the edge of the bottom pool. Make sure that the liner has both the length and width to reach the far extent of the header pool with enough overlap

at the end and sides so that you can make any slight corrections to the level later on. If the header pool is much wider than the stream, it would be better to order two separate pieces of liner, rather than waste too wide a piece for the length of the stream.

7 So that the waterfall has a natural link with the base pool and a good foundation, you will need to start building the base of the waterfall from the marginal shelf in the bottom pool. This will be subjected to extra weight, so place a spare offcut of liner on the bottom pool shelf to protect it. Then build up with either one large stone or two smaller foundation stones, placing them tightly against the overlapping liner from the stream, which was left draped over the edge. If the waterfall foundation stones are not stable, you will have to drain the base pool to the level of the marginal shelf and mortar the foundation stones to the marginal shelf for strength.

8 Pack stiff mortar between the foundation stone and the overlapping piece of liner. To further increase the stability, roll up the liner tightly over the top of the foundation stone and pack mortar behind the liner and the earth bank.

9 The next stone to be fixed is the spillstone, over which the water will flow. Partly unroll the liner again so that you can place a suitable stone on top of the foundation stone. Choose a flat stone and make sure that the front edge of the stone overlaps the foundation stone and the water in the bottom pool. Mortar this stone into position, checking with a watering can that the water flows as you want it to.

ROCKY STREAM AND WATERFALL

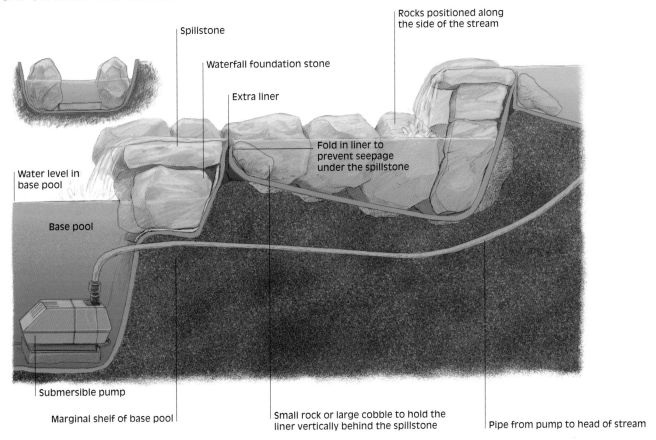

Spillstone

Waterfall foundation stone

Extra liner

Rocks positioned along the side of the stream

Fold in liner to prevent seepage under the spillstone

Water level in base pool

Base pool

Submersible pump

Marginal shelf of base pool

Small rock or large cobble to hold the liner vertically behind the spillstone

Pipe from pump to head of stream

10 Now build side walls around the spillstone, securing these with mortar to the liner if necessary so that they are perfectly stable. Build up the rocks so that they are higher than the spillstone and will direct the stream water towards this central stone.

11 To stop the stream water seeping under the spillstone, pleat the liner to form a lip behind the spillstone, folding the liner so that the top of the lip finishes at the same height as the top of the stone. Mortar a small stone to this pleat to wedge it in place.

12 The liner can now be unrolled along the length of the stream and rocks placed on the liner along both sides. Make sure that the tops of the rocks are higher than the spillstone. Do not pull up the liner

behind these rocks until all the rocks are in position.

13 Repeat the process at the waterfall that forms the junction of the header pool to the stream, using the same liner under the waterfall stones as before.

14 The header pool is edged with rocks in the same way as the stream. Make sure that their tops are higher than the level of the waterfall spillstone.

15 Bury the flexible pipe from the pump in a trench 60–90cm (2–3ft) from the watercourse and drape it over a rock at the side of the header pool. If you wish to be able to make adjustments to the rate of flow, you can fit a small flow regulator into the pipe just before it enters the header pool. Place

another rock on top of the pipe to conceal it.

16 Pull up the liner vertically behind all the rocks and wedge it in place with compacted soil on the outside. Do not trim the liner until you have tested the stream.

17 Turn on the pump in the base pool and check the sides for overflow. If satisfied, trim the liner and hide the edge in the soil. Remember that the edge of the liner must be above the water level throughout the course of the stream.

18 Gaps between the edging rocks and the liner can be filled with soil and planted with suitable small marginals or moisture-loving plants. Place small rocks or pebbles on the floor of the stream to disguise the liner.

CANAL

Think of a long, narrow, straight, shallow pool and you could have a canal. As with many still-water features, the edging makes or breaks the effect, and great attention should be given to its style. The width will be dictated by the size of garden and its surroundings. Paving would work as an edge to a canal in a lawn to contrast with the grass. In a paved area, bricks or setts would be more suitable.

Although canals or rills are most often seen in a paved setting in domestic gardens, they can look superb when introduced into a long formal lawn. A canal can be an excellent way of accentuating a focal point in a garden or making a bold division between areas. A canal can also make clever use of reflections, and one running parallel to the house can have some quite unusual reflective qualities.

This project requires some skill in bricklaying and the use of mortar. Because the edges play such an important part in the overall appearance of the feature, their mortaring together must be done skilfully. If your skills are borderline, use edging materials that are long and large so that the number of joints is reduced to a minimum. It may be possible to brush dry mortar into the joints and add the water carefully with a fine rose on a watering can. Never flood the joints with too much water or the mortar stain will seep out from between the paving slabs.

Tools & equipment

Spade
Wheelbarrow
Rake
Spirit level and straight-edge
Level pegs
String
Mortaring pointed trowel (and
   plasterer's trowel if skimming
   method used, see step 10)

CANAL

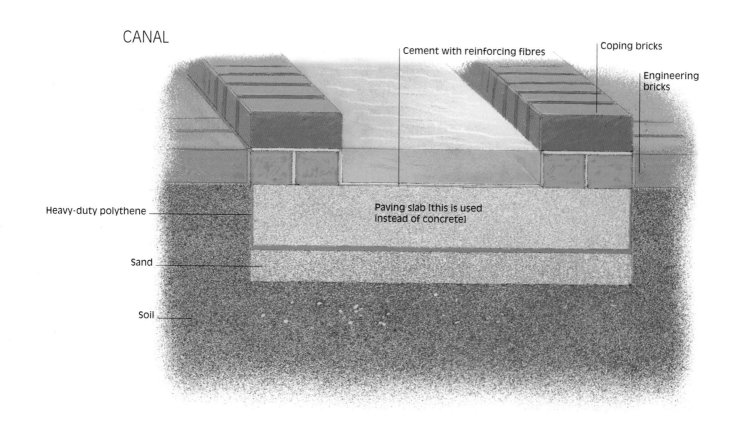

Cement with reinforcing fibres

Coping bricks

Engineering bricks

Heavy-duty polythene

Paving slab [this is used instead of concrete]

Sand

Soil

Materials

Soft sand

Heavy-duty polythene sheet (if a liner is not used)

Ready-mixed mortar

Paving slabs, 90 x 60 x 5cm (36 x 24 x 2in)

Engineering bricks

Walling blocks

Flexible liner (if liner method is used for waterproofing)

Mortar reinforcing fibres (for skimming method only, see step 10)

1 Mark out the length and width of the proposed canal. This canal uses 90 x 60cm (3 x 2ft) paving slabs as the base, with the long side of the slab laid across the canal. The trench needs to be dug about 15cm (6in) wider than the slabs, which makes it easier to lay them level. If the canal is to be constructed in an existing paved area, remove the paving stones carefully, including the slabs that will be adjacent to the canal. Check that the canal will be level along its entire length by knocking in pegs along the side of the proposed line. Use a spirit level and straight-edge to check that the tops of all the pegs are perfectly level. Leave the pegs in place as a check when you are building up the shallow sides of the canal.

2 Dig out a straight-sided trench to a depth of 45cm (18in).

3 Place a layer of soft sand on the bottom of the trench to a depth of 5–8cm (2–3in).

4 Lay the slabs as close as possible to each other and keep them perfectly level across and along the line of the canal. Check with a spirit level as you lay each slab.

5 There are several ways in which you can build and waterproof the sides; two of these are described here, the first using a flexible liner.

6 Mortar a line of the wide concrete walling blocks that have hollow portions inside along both sides of the paving slabs.

7 Lay the liner neatly into the base of the canal then arrange it over the top of the walling block, leaving ample overlap so that it can eventually be taken under and behind the thickness of a brick laid at right angles to the canal.

8 Mortar waterproof, navy blue engineering bricks on top of the liner, with the wide concrete walling block underneath, so that there is about 2.5cm (1in) overlap on the inside of the canal. The bricks should be laid at right angles to the line of the canal and butted together with mortar. These will form the top of the canal and must be laid perfectly level. Keep checking this with a spirit level or a taut level string connected to level pegs at the ends of the canal. Leave the mortar to dry.

9 The following weekend pack sand into the gap outside the canal sides and secure the liner, which should be trimmed level to the top of the edging brick and held upright with paving or turf. By taking the liner up and behind the canal edging brick, the water level can be allowed to reach the top of the brick, which looks much better than when it is lower than this.

10 Instead of using a flexible liner, the base and walls of the inside of the canal can be rendered with a thin layer of mortar, which has had reinforcing fibres added to the mix. These fibres add considerable strength to the mortar lining and make it capable of resisting any slight movement of the base or walls. The mortar reinforcing fibres are available by mail order from large water garden suppliers and are strongly recommended if you are waterproofing any rigid water feature with a mortar rendering.

11 The canal ends can be closed with walls built at right angles in the same way as the side walls.

12 Moving canals rely on a pump for circulation, so they must be level and incorporate a pipe at each end to circulate the water. They must also retain water when the pump is off. Sometimes the water at the outlet will enter a cascade or weir where the water returns to a reservoir. The pump returns the water to a hidden pipe introduced into the canal source or a pool at a higher level, which pours water into the end of the canal.

Below The impact of this canal is cleverly extended by a gap in the hedge that leads the eye into the rest of the garden beyond.

There are numerous ways in which a water feature can be made more attractive by adding sometimes quite small details. The following ideas are just a few of the ways to enhance your water feature.

SPECIAL FEATURES

Special Features

EDGING A FORMAL POOL

Simple edges have been recommended wherever possible as they are easy to construct and achievable within a limited time. Often, of course, the simplest edge is the most satisfactory, and most will stand the test of time. Nonetheless, when you have extra time, you may want to construct something more durable or complicated, and this is especially likely with a formal pool.

Right An outdoor room where the small pool with its hidden filtration becomes a source of cooling refreshment.

Below The dark coping enables the water to reflect the strong shapes of containers and plants more effectively.

A formal pool must have a crisp, sharply defined edge. It must be well built and perfectly level so that the true horizontal line of the water is parallel with the horizontal lines of the lower and upper edges of the paving around it. If a small pool is edged in the same type of paving that was used for the large patio on which it is built, the pool can be dwarfed: it would be better with a contrasting surround to give it more emphasis. This is where smaller materials can be effective, especially weather-resistant decorative bricks, engineering bricks, setts and brick pavers, which are brick-like but are made of concrete rather than of clay.

Bricks

Small circular pools are difficult to edge because the material has to allow for a curving edge. Bricks are an ideal choice for this type of position, especially if they have a rolled edge on the side facing the water. Engineering bricks are suitable for highlighting edges, as they are weatherproof and their colour blends with water and most other paving colours. If you prefer decorative housebricks, check they are frost resistant. The bricks may be in contact with water, and it is vital that they are not going to crumble in the first frost.

Setts

Granite and sandstone setts are good for edging small pools and for curves. Makers have begun to produce some very good substitutes in concrete. These setts are generally charcoal in colour, which is very easy to match.

EDGING FOR A FORMAL POOL

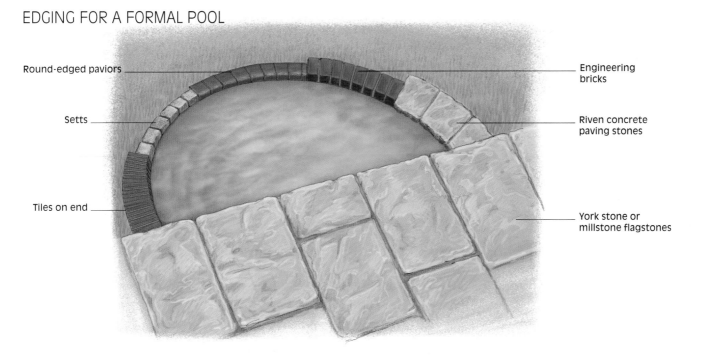

Round-edged paviors

Setts

Tiles on end

Engineering bricks

Riven concrete paving stones

York stone or millstone flagstones

Timber

Formal pools can also be edged satisfactorily with timber, and this looks particularly attractive if the surface beyond the immediate pool edge is grass. Timber tiles, log roll, sleepers and timber planks can all be used to create straight and curved edges. Timber has a more limited life than concrete or stone. Wherever possible, use pressure-treated wood, and if you are prepared to carry out regular maintenance to prevent a build up of algae, there is a softness and warmth to timber that is particularly appealing, especially in the plantsperson's garden.

Safety

The surface of any hard edging around a pool must be non-slip. If paving slabs are used, they should have a riven surface and be kept clear of algae. Many reconstituted concrete paving slabs are now made with roughened surfaces, and these make ideal edging for a formal pool. Decking planks and tiles are also now available with ridged and ribbed surfaces, and these should be used in all circumstances because timber will quickly become slimy and very dangerous.

Left The timber surround, despite the formal shape, is a sympathetic edge to the heavily planted border.

EDGING AN INFORMAL POOL

There is a wide variety of materials to exploit as edging for informal pools, and the great advantage of informality is that it is not necessary to use the same material all the way around the pool as is the case in a more formal situation.

There is, in fact, an advantage to varying the edges of an informal pool, especially to avoid marring the natural look of a pool by surrounding it with a narrow ribbon of crazy paving that is all the same width.

It is useful if a part of the edge visited frequently is paved in some way. If there are fish in the pool, feeding will take place from the same point, and this is a good place to lay substantial paving slabs as edging. The rest of the perimeter can be created from one or more of the more common but less stable edges, such as grass, rocks, plants, cobbles or timber.

Grass

A lawn or grass edge is a natural-looking edge to an informal pool. There are two main problems to overcome when grass is used, however. If the edge is vulnerable to frequent and heavy wear, it could crumble badly and even sink slightly into a pool made with a flexible liner. This can be overcome by making a solid edge to the pool with concrete blocks, bricks or walling blocks, which are placed on the outside of the liner so that the tops of the support are 5–8cm (2–3in) under the grass. This will allow the grass to continue to grow but will stop it sliding towards the pool.

Above Small washed rounded pebbles make a good buffer between grass and water and allow any variation in level to look quite natural.

Right The most natural looking edge of all is plants. Here a bed of moisture-lovers has been made at the pool side.

The other problem with a grass edge is to stop it creeping into the water, where the mower cannot reach. A good way to prevent this is to use a length of timber, such as log roll, to form an edge between the water and the grass. Keep the top of the log roll below grass level or the mower will be unable to reach the edge of the grass and strimming would cause the cuttings to fly into the water.

Rocks

An edging of rocks can be most successful, particularly when the rocks are partially submerged and appear to be natural outcrops because their tops are arranged at parallel angles. If there is a rocky water course spilling into the pool, it is a natural extension of the watercourse to use the same type of rock on both the watercourse and the pool surround. Again, it will look better if the rocks form only a part of the pool edge and do not totally circumscribe the pool. When you are building this type of edge you should make sure that there is a wide enough marginal shelf for the rocks to sit on, and to give extra stability to the rocks, bed them on a base of stiff mortar.

Marginals

The most natural-looking edge of all is when marginal plants are allowed to mimic the appearance of a natural pool. Beyond the marginal plants the vegetation changes gradually to moisture-loving plants and then to plants that naturally thrive in drier conditions. This type of arrangement can be created artificially by having a soil bed next to the pool, which is kept moist with a lining of polythene, punctured at the bottom to allow slow drainage. These areas are often referred to as bog gardens, although they are strictly not bogs as some drainage is made possible (see the informal bog area on pages 80–81). These beds of moisture-loving plants make access to the pool side difficult, but they are ideal for forming part edges, especially as they make the pool seem larger than it is.

BRIDGES

Bridges are appropriate for small water features only if there is some purpose to them and the construction is kept quite simple. Too often bridges are added that are quite out of proportion to the pool. In small Oriental-style gardens, bridges should not be painted red as this makes them too overwhelming relative to the pool and other features.

The arched bridge can also look out of place over a very small pool or stream, when the arch is so severe in gradient that it becomes more of an obstacle than an aid to crossing water. If you want to make an arched bridge, make the gradient of the arch as gentle and restful as possible, taking the ends of the bridge well beyond the edge of the pool or stream.

A simple bridge can be a most inviting feature, and if it is linked to a path of stepping stones, grass or paving at each end to provide a purposeful route around the garden, it will be most successful. Railway sleepers, laid in a group of two or three, can be used to make the simplest of bridges, but they may be too heavy and thick for a very small pool. A neater bridge can be made by using two supporting joists of timber, 15 x 5cm (6 x 2in), crossing the pool with decking planks screwed at right angles to the joists. Provide a foundation at each end of the bridge on which the joists will rest – a paving stone, for instance, which is slightly higher than the soil – making sure that it is level with the one on the other side. Use pressure-treated timber and be meticulous about removing algae.

Above Simple planks running along rather than across the bridge lead the eye to the seat in the distance and encourage you to walk across.

Right The gentle gradient of this arch adds elegance to the view rather than acting as an obstacle as it might if the arch were higher.

Tools & equipment

Spade
Shovel
Spirit level and straight-edge
Screwdriver
Wheelbarrow
Watering can

Materials

Rough planed timber for joists, 15 x 5cm (6 x 2in)

Galvanized 12cm (5in) brackets with 5cm (2in) galvanized bolts and nuts

Countersunk 8-gauge screws 5cm (2in) long

Cross-plank timber 15 x 2.5cm (6 x 1in)

3 x 25kg bags of ready-mixed concrete

1 A bridge built with the timbers specified should not exceed 2.4m (8ft) in length without a central pier or further support. A minimum width of 60cm (2ft) is adequate and in proportion to a small water feature.

2 Firm foundations should be built at least 23cm (9in) from the water's edge so that the sloping sides of the pool do not affect their stability.

3 For a short bridge less than 1.2m (4ft) long, a paving stone mortared on to hardcore would be an adequate foundation. A longer bridge needs the strength of concrete blocks.

4 Thè concrete blocks can be made by creating rough rectangular moulds, 75 x 20 x 10cm (30 x 8in x 4in), using rough timbers nailed together.

5 Position these moulds at either side of the proposed crossing point, checking that their tops are level with each other with a spirit level placed on top of a straight-edge. Pour ready-mixed concrete mix into the moulds.

6 Before the concrete sets, set the two joists that will support the bridge 20cm (8in) apart on the moist concrete. The joists should be 10 x 5cm (4 x 2in) by the length of the bridge. Holding 12cm (5in) galvanized angle brackets against the joists over the concrete, mark the moist concrete with the positions to sink in two galvanized bolts, each 5cm (2in) long. Embed these into the concrete with the screw end protruding by 2.5cm (1in). Bolt the brackets onto the bolts when the concrete is set.

7 Remove the timber moulds and screw the joists to the brackets. Lay the cross-planks over the joists at right angles to them. The cross-planks are made of 15 x 2.5cm (6 x 1in) timber, which have been pre-cut before screwing them on to the joists in 60cm (2ft) lengths. Leave a gap of 1cm (½in) between the cross-planks to allow the timber space to expand when wet.

BRIDGE

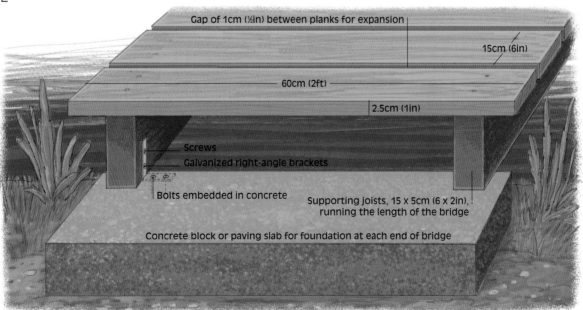

Gap of 1cm (½in) between planks for expansion

15cm (6in)

60cm (2ft)

2.5cm (1in)

Screws

Galvanized right-angle brackets

Bolts embedded in concrete

Supporting joists, 15 x 5cm (6 x 2in), running the length of the bridge

Concrete block or paving slab for foundation at each end of bridge

STEPPING STONES

The effect of stepping stones is enhanced considerably when they are linked to a path on the ground at either side of the pool or stream. This is especially effective if the path itself consists of stepping stones set into a lawn. Even quite a small pool can be made more interesting by adding one or two stepping stones into the water. They must, of course, be level and kept free of slippery algae.

Above The central stones here are lower than those near the pool edge, adding a sense of height to the composition.

Right An informal and strikingly bold arrangement of thin pieces of York stone over shallow water.

Formal stepping stones

Formal stepping stones are very effective if made in the same material as the paving around the pool, thus adding continuity to the design. There may be room for only one stone, which need not be in the dead centre but may look better slightly off-centre. You should only consider using stepping stones if the water is less than 45cm (18in) deep. The stepping stone should be set with its surface about 10cm (4in) above the water level and it should have a minimum diameter of 60cm (2ft).

If you are adding stepping stones to an existing pool, drain the water and try to keep as much of it as possible in containers while the job is being done. Place a paving stone that is at least the size of the stepping stone to be used above the water on a 5cm (2in) bed of mortar on the bottom of the pool and tap it level. When the mortar has set build up a pier of engineering bricks to just above the water surface. The bricks must be kept level as the courses are mortared together. Four bricks at right angles to each other make a suitable pier for a 60cm (2ft) slab. You should not need more than four or five courses of bricks in the pier with mortar between the courses. The paving slab is mortared squarely on top of the pier and checked to make

sure it is level. After two or three days the mortar will be hard enough to reintroduce water into the pool.

Informal stepping stones

Informal stepping stones can be made with flat-topped, irregular boulders, partially submerged in the shallow margins of a pool or stream. Boulders large enough to stand on will be heavy to lift, so get help. Drain the pool or stream to just below the depth where the boulder will sit, and set the boulder on a thick layer of stiff mortar. Allow this to dry for a day or two before reintroducing the water. The ideal setting for this type of stepping stone is a stream, where it provides a naturalistic crossing point and creates interesting eddying effects in the water.

There are some effective informally shaped stepping stones made in concrete, which could be used instead of boulders. These have to be carefully constructed so that the pier supporting the stepping stone is not visible above the waterline. Large timber slices can be used as informal stepping stones in places like bog gardens. Pieces of natural stone shaped like crazy paving can also be used as stepping stones but as they risk breaking near any sharp points, they should only be used over shallow water and have several supports underneath each piece. Avoid using soft sandstone and ensure that the underside of the stone is clear of the water so that it can dry out after rain and be less susceptible to frost damage.

Above To add emphasis to the stepping stones and link them with the rest of the garden, the colour of the insert tiles is continued across the water to the other side.

COBBLE BEACHES

Although they are usually thought of as a type of edging for informal pools, cobble beaches also deserve a special mention because they are not only an attractive feature in their own right but they also provide a superb ramp for the entry and departure of wildlife – breeding frogs, newts and toads, or birds wanting a cooling drink or bath – to the pool.

A beach makes life very much easier for amphibians, like newts, frogs and toads, as they can move in and out of the water, which also warms up more readily over the shallow cobbles and lures fish and other creatures to sunbathe.

The natural beach effect can be made even more attractive when it is sparsely planted with occasional clump-forming or spreading plants.

The gentler the gradient, the less risk there is that the cobbles will roll to the pool bottom. If an existing pool with a flexible liner was not built with a shallow slope, it may be possible once the pool is partly drained to lift the liner and re-contour the slope by adding soil beneath the liner and underlay, which should then be replaced. These instructions assume that you are adapting an existing pond.

Materials

Sifted topsoil (if needed)
Ready-mixed mortar
Washed cobbles of various sizes
Clump-forming or spreading
    plants

Tools & equipment

Spade or trowel
Hosepipe for marking out
Plasterer's trowel

COBBLE BEACH

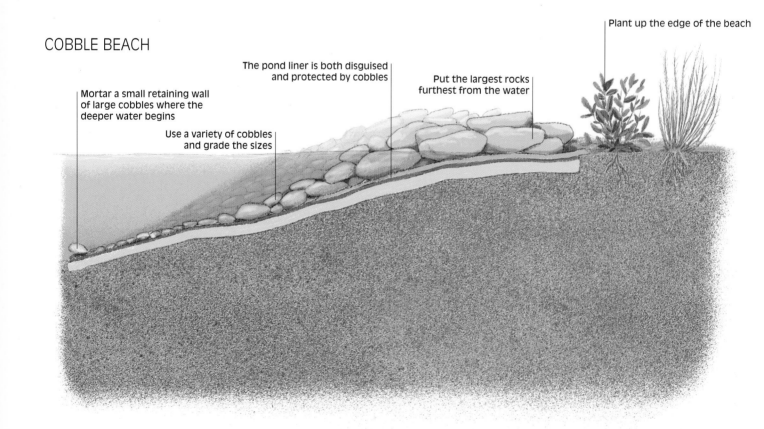

Plant up the edge of the beach

Mortar a small retaining wall of large cobbles where the deeper water begins

Use a variety of cobbles and grade the sizes

The pond liner is both disguised and protected by cobbles

Put the largest rocks furthest from the water

1 Drain the pool by about 40cm (16in), moving any fish and marginal plants to temporary homes if necessary.

2 Mortar a group of large cobbles on top of the liner in a rough line, which will be about 30cm (12in) deep when the water is replaced. Also mortar larger cobbles onto the line nearer the eventual water level. This will keep them stable and the mortar will protect the liner from sharp objects such as dogs' claws.

3 Allow the mortar to harden for a day or two before spreading cobbles from the lower batter to just above the final water line. Use the smallest cobbles underwater, saving the larger ones for the area above the waterline.

4 The beach area above the waterline can be extended for two to three metres (yards) to allow large boulders and planting to be interspersed.

5 Refill the pond and put back the fish and marginal plants.

DECKING

Decking is not just a good choice as a type of edging for a pool, but it also introduces a large area for outdoor living as an alternative to hard paving in a patio area. As well as being a highly ornamental surface, it has many practical advantages over paving or concrete, as it is easier to create different levels, and forms a sympathetic edging to an expanse of water.

The design of the decking edge allows the water to be overlapped by timbers, creating the impression that the water passes underneath and thereby making the pool seem larger. The piers for decking can be extended into shallow water to create jetties.

Decking can be made of decking tiles or decking planks, lengths of timber, 3–4m (10–13ft) long and 15–20cm (6–8in) wide, with ribbed surfaces. The decking tiles are normally 45cm (18in) square and can be arranged with the timbers fixed across the frame diagonally or at right angles.

Buy only pressure-treated timber with a minimum thickness of 2.5cm (1in) for the decking planks. If you use thinner timber you will have to increase the number of cross-supports under the deck to prevent warping. Several types of timber are used for decking, from the more expensive hardwoods to some very cheap softwoods. It pays to shop around for such an expensive waterside feature, because both longevity and the quality of the construction are at stake. Decking surfaces should be kept meticulously scrubbed and free from algae. The ribbed surface helps to prevent slipping but the surface of the ribs can be quite lethal once they are coated in green algae.

An existing pool will have a bearing on the site and size of a decking platform. Because it is likely to be a popular surface for outdoor events, make the proposed area as large as you can afford. An existing patio with paving slabs that have been down for some time will make an excellent solid and level base for the decking. This project assumes that you do not have a paved base.

Above A sympathetic mixture of materials and plants in a small area where decking makes the ideal centrepiece.

Left A decking island is cleverly enhanced by the arrangement of the planks in a series of concentric squares.

Opposite The decking has been extended cleverly by making stepping stones, which appear to float on the water, in the same timber.

Tools & equipment

Spade
Rake
Spirit level and straight-edge
Saw
Screwdriver
Hammer

Materials

Pea shingle
Tanalized timber for bearers, 5 x 8cm (2 x 3in)
Decking planks 120 x 32mm (4¾ x 1¼in)
Pre-cast concrete decking foundation pads
Galvanized 8-gauge 5cm (2in) screws
Fascia board for edges

Below The ribbed surfacing of the decking planks is an attractive alternative to plain wood and also helps to prevent slipping.

DECKING

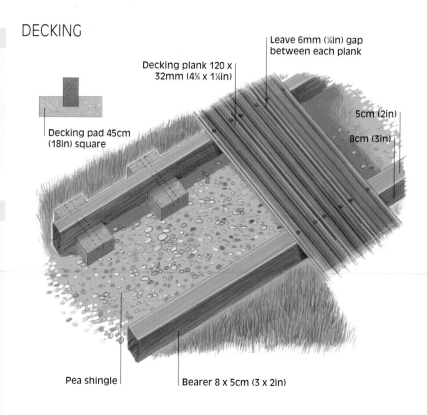

Decking pad 45cm (18in) square

Decking plank 120 x 32mm (4¾ x 1¼in)

Leave 6mm (¼in) gap between each plank

5cm (2in)

8cm (3in)

Pea shingle

Bearer 8 x 5cm (3 x 2in)

1 Clear the site of weeds, using a spot-treatment for deep-rooted perennial weeds.

2 Rake the site level, then spread pea shingle over the surface.

3 The decking tiles or planks will sit on supporting timbers known as bearers or joists, which are normally made of 8 x 5cm (3 x 2in) tanalized timber and are placed 75cm (30in) apart at right angles to the line of the decking planks. The bearers need to be set on pre-cast concrete decking pads, 45cm (18in) square and 10cm (4in) thick, which are placed 1.2m (4ft) apart. These decking pads have been grooved so that the timber rests securely in the channel inside the pad. Check that the pads are level with a spirit level and straight-edge.

4 Alternatively, the bearers can be bedded on firm soil in excavated channels containing hardcore covered with a 5cm (2in) layer of sand. If necessary, bricks can be used on top of the sand to compensate for any major changes in level. Check with a spirit level that the bearers are level and make sure that they are rigid. Secure any slightly wobbly bearers by nailing them to posts driven into the soil underneath.

5 When the bearers are firm and level, the decking planks can be screwed onto the bearers. The decking planks should be 32mm (1¼in) thick. Although thinner planks are available, these have a tendency to warp, and if the bearers are not close enough, you will feel a slight 'give' when you walk on them. The planks are 120mm (4¾in) wide and grooved on the upper surface.

6 When you screw the planks onto the bearers leave a 6mm (¼in) gap between each plank to allow for expansion.

7 To avoid 'cupping', a slight curve in the plank at the sides that occurs when only one screw is used in the centre of a plank, use two screws at each bearer – in the grooves of the plank close to the edges.

8 When all the planks are screwed down and the edges are cut to size, screw a timber fascia board vertically to the ends of the bearers to hide the rough ends of the wood from a side view.

9 If you wish, the fascia board can be wide enough to extend down to any adjacent waterline so that the edge of a flexible liner is hidden behind it.

10 Check finally that no screw tops have been left proud of the decking surface because the wooden surface is a natural attraction to walking barefoot.

Special Features

DRIED RIVER BEDS AND GRAVEL BEDS

The setting of a water feature is as important as the feature itself, and many of the small fountain features look good when they are surrounded by the free design of gravel beds, perhaps interspersed with boulders in a variety of sizes, colours and textures that help to create a more realistic look. Looking at how stones are distributed in a natural river bed will help you to decide where to place larger rocks.

Right A gravel bed, primarily designed for its texture and lack of maintenance can soon be the platform for creating the appearance of a dried-up stream bed.

It is sometimes difficult to know where to start with an area of gravel, which can look quite alien in some soft green settings. Gravel areas tend to be more appropriate for sunnier, drier climates where the planting is sparser and of more drought-resistant species. Such a setting can be just the place to introduce the refreshment of water in the same way that it refreshed early Islamic gardens. Emerging from an expanse of lawn, a gravel bed might be the place to introduce all sorts of water features that would otherwise be lost in a large, meticulously striped lawn.

Siting

If nibbling away at the sides of your garden is not your style, why not consider building a dried river bed to run right through it? If there is a slight slope, so much the better, because the river bed can start quite narrow at the higher end and gradually widen as it progresses to the lower part of the garden. A variety of features can be placed within this setting, ranging from cobble and millstone fountains to lined areas near the wider section, where lusher and taller moisture-loving plants can be grown.

Alternatively, the water features can be made first, and as time permits the area allocated to a gravel river bed can be developed gradually. The grass should be removed, and the proposed bed lined with a semi-permeable membrane designed to stop weeds growing up through it but at the same time allowing water through. Different sizes of gravel or cobbles should be arranged over the membrane, with the smaller sizes in the centre and the larger cobbles towards the sides.

Planting

Planting can be done by making X-shaped slits in the membrane. It will look more realistic if smaller plants are used in the narrower section, with taller plants where the bed widens out. Ornamental grasses, such as *Stipa gigantea* and *Carex* spp., are suitable for such a feature, which allows a more flexible approach to planting than a more disciplined border or patio.

The illusion of a dried-up river bed can be heightened by the addition of a bridge, river-washed boulders, driftwood and timber, placed at random.

LIGHTING

There is no garden feature so appropriate for lighting as a water feature. Lighting can give a water feature a completely different feel at night than it has during the day. If the water is moving, light brings a sparkle to the movement; if the water is still, the lighting can bring to an inky black surface reflections that you never even knew existed.

Many of the water features described in this book require electricity to power a submersible pump, so the expense of bringing the supply into the garden will already have been met if the lighting uses mains electricity.

Safety

Safety regulations are being constantly tightened in the garden, and all electrical equipment must be protected by a residual current device (RCD, sometimes known as a contact circuit breaker). The trip switches in RCDs are extremely responsive, and electrical storms or power cuts often cause them to trip. If the lighting does not come on, check first that this device is not the cause.

Regulations are increasingly leaning towards the use of low-voltage lighting wherever possible in the garden. Fortunately, low-voltage electricity is easier to install than mains voltage cable, but does require a transformer, which can be an indoor model or a special waterproof type for outdoor use.

Benefits of lighting a pool

One of the main benefits of outdoor lighting is the opportunity that it offers to provide a light source from a completely different direction or even in a different colour. Water lighting needs a careful choice of type of lens, position and colour.

Opposite Simple lighting gives this bowl an almost space-age feel.

Left Lighting can be used to enhance the most baroque of features.

USES OF LOW VOLTAGE LIGHTING IN THE GARDEN

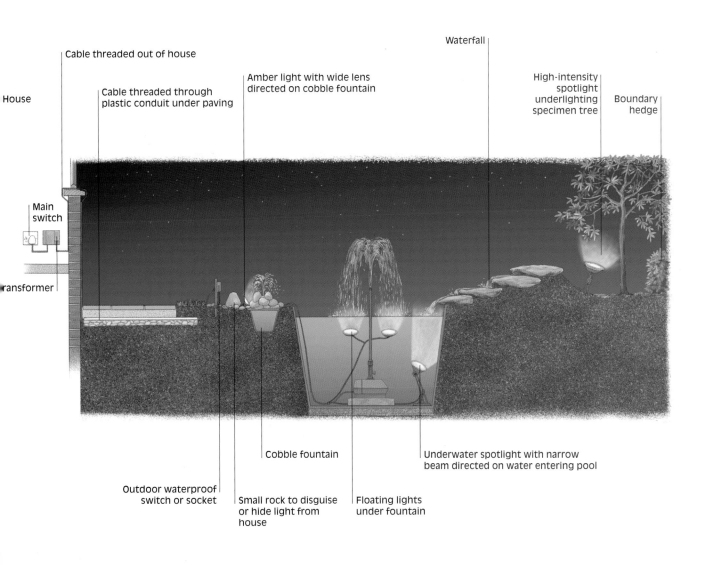

Cable threaded out of house

House

Cable threaded through plastic conduit under paving

Amber light with wide lens directed on cobble fountain

Waterfall

High-intensity spotlight underlighting specimen tree

Boundary hedge

Main switch

Transformer

Outdoor waterproof switch or socket

Cobble fountain

Small rock to disguise or hide light from house

Floating lights under fountain

Underwater spotlight with narrow beam directed on water entering pool

Many of the projects described in this book involve small fountain features, and the part of the feature that will be most responsive to lighting is the moving water. Decide whether it will be best illuminated from the side, from above, or from underneath, which is often most effective. Think also about the focus of the light: a narrow fountain spout can be highlighted by a lens below the spout that appears to restrict the beam of light into the water with an almost uncanny effect. On the other hand, a fountain spout may need the wall mask to be highlighted, so that a slightly wider beam is required, but still most effectively used from below.

Lighting moving water

When the light source is introduced from under the water, movement on the water surface is brought into play. If this surface movement is turbulent, the ripple effect of the seemingly

Practicalities

Using Light in the Water Garden

The following guidelines will help you make a start in exploring the full potential of lighting water features.

• Avoid large, clumsy lights with casings that are so conspicuous in the day that they spoil the daylight scene. Choose small, black, non-shiny casings and hide these behind boulders or plants.

• If you are using underwater lights make sure that the water is clear, or the green water will be exaggerated by the light.

• Direct the light away from the main viewing area so that people do not look into a light.

• For a reflective pool, underlight a feature such as a tree or sculpture on the opposite side of a still pool from the main viewpoint. This prevents light from catching the water, which could occur from a light that is positioned on the viewing side of the water.

• Avoid the use of too many coloured lenses. White or amber light works well with water. The water spout of a cobble fountain can dance like a flame when it is lit with an amber spotlight.

• For the best mix of shadow and texture on a smooth object like an urn, light from the side and at a slight upward angle.

moving light is particularly effective reflected onto expansive, flat surfaces such as walls or canopies. Falling spouts from fountains are effective in producing this turbulence over an underwater light positioned at the base of the fountain, but it can also be achieved by a light under a waterfall. This not only highlights the falling water but can bring alive the extraordinary beauty and delicacy of a fern frond clinging to the back of the waterfall, which is normally hidden in the shade in daylight.

Above Complex features, with a number of different textures and colours are better suited to fairly simple lighting.

Water will always be an attraction to some form of wildlife and the open pools featured in the two and three weekend projects are large enough to support a small population of ornamental fish.

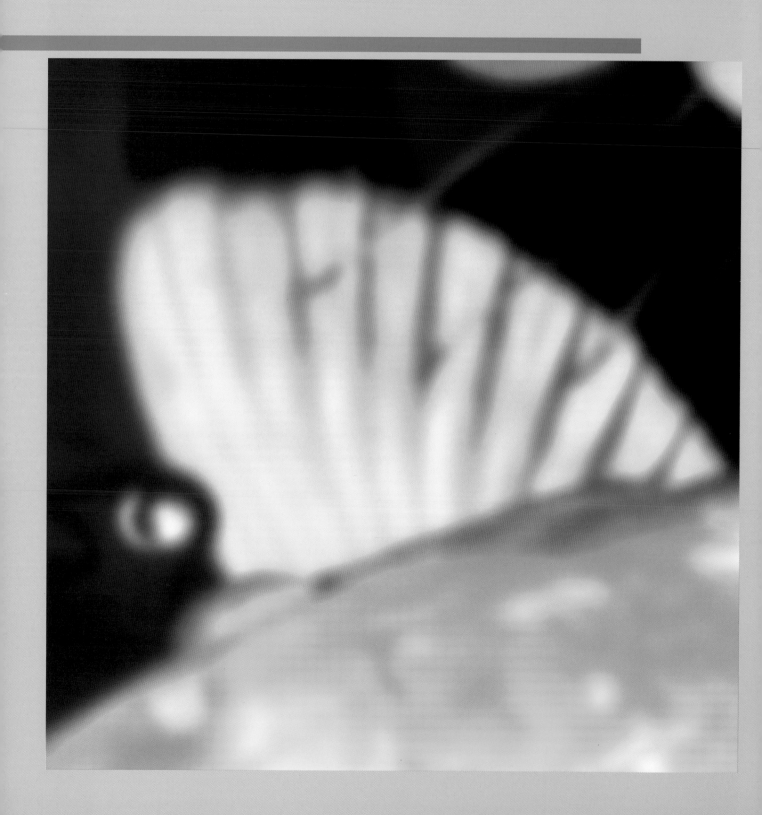

FISH AND OTHER WILDLIFE

Fish and Other Wildlife

CHOOSING FISH

There is no denying the pleasure that pet goldfish can bring. As with all pets, however, care needs to be taken in preparing a suitable environment and in selecting the number and type of fish for a particular water feature. For instance, it would be cruel to keep a large koi in a small barrel, but overstocking a pond with smaller fish or not providing oxygen will also lead to stress and disease.

Above Golden orfe are ideal for helping to control midge larvae on the surface.

Right Comet goldfish, one of the most attractive of the fancy goldfish, are a little slower than the common goldfish when predators are about.

A rough guide of 2.5cm (1in) of body length for every 0.09 sq m (1 sq ft) of surface area is often used to help determine the number of fish that can be stocked. This quantity is for a new pool, and an established, well-planted pool could probably cope with double this length per area. The guideline assumes a minimum pool depth of 45cm (18in), and although fish can be kept in water shallower than this, the guideline would no longer apply and there would probably be a need for supplementary aeration or filtration. For instance, a trough or barrel used as a water feature would support no more than a couple of small fish, each about 5cm (2in) long unless extra oxygen was introduced by a fountain or waterfall.

Suitable fish

The type of fish chosen is also important as some are more tolerant than others. If the available space is border-line for fish welfare and there is space to house only two or three fish adequately, goldfish would have to be the choice because of their sheer adaptability and toughness.

When a pool is large enough to house fish without any qualms for their welfare, there is much to be said for a mixed community of ornamental fish to allow their different habits and characteristics to be observed. A fish community of three species – goldfish, orfe and koi – would be a good choice, because they feed at different levels and most mixes of fish food will be suitable for all three types.

Goldfish need little introduction: orange-red in colour, they grow to about 15cm (6in) and have a lifespan of 10 years. They are among the most temperature-tolerant of fish and are fairly resistant to some of the disorders associated with the more exotic fish types. Several fancy forms with long tails and fins have been bred, but some of them are not entirely hardy.

Golden orfe, a favourite European fish with a lifespan of 15–20 years, is noted for its speed in the shallows, where its sleek body with a golden sheen darts for insects on the surface. The active habit of the fish, which can grow to 30–50cm (12–20in), means that it should be given ample room and is suitable only for pools with a minimum surface area of 4.6 sq m (50 sq ft). Orfe need highly oxygenated water and will be among the first to suffer on hot summer evenings when oxygen levels are low.

Koi are now more commonplace and available in a wide variety of colour markings. They are fine in a small water feature when they are young, but as they can eventually reach 60cm (2ft), you will have to move them to bigger pools when they become too large.

Buying and introducing fish

It is better to buy several smaller fish than fewer larger ones, because young fish will settle in more quickly. Make sure that there is a good plant cover so that the fish don't get nervous and damage themselves. Buy them in late spring if possible, when plants are in full growth and there is a greater variety of live food. If they are introduced in autumn, they have little time to build up body reserves before their first winter outdoors.

Most ornamental fish are imported and before their journey to the wholesaler, they are fed on foodstuffs that increase their colouring in order to make them more attractive. Avoid fish that are highly coloured, as this indicates that they have spent too little time since leaving the breeder to have settled down and got used to a new climate. It is always best for both plants and fish to buy from a source with a reputation to lose and, although this may mean slightly more expensive purchases, it will be more sensible in the long term.

The most traumatic time for the fish is the transportation from the supplier to your pool, and it is best to enclose them in a plastic bag with some shallow water and filled with neat oxygen before being sealed. The bag should be placed in a tall cardboard box and kept covered until you get home. The fish should be all right for at least the remainder of the day in these conditions, but try to keep the box out of direct sunshine, especially when it is inside a car.

When you get home, float the bag for a couple of hours in the pool so that the temperature of the water in the bag can get closer to the temperature of the water in the pool, then release the sealed end and let the fish swim out. Do not tip them out.

Practicalities

Cleaning the pool

If the pool has to be emptied for cleaning, the welfare of the fish is a major concern, particularly in warm weather. Have ready a temporary tank or pool – a child's paddling pool is ideal – as a short-term home. Pump out or siphon off some of the pond water into the temporary pool to minimize shock to the fish. Net as many of the fish as possible before the mud gets stirred up. As the water level drops, remove the plants, placing the oxygenators and floaters in the temporary pool with the fish to give them some cover. If the fish show extreme distress – gulping at the surface or going over on their sides – run a fountain kit or place an oxygenating air block designed for aquaria in the water.

Above Easily trained to eat out of your hand, the koi remains as popular as ever.

CARING FOR FISH

Once the fish have been introduced to the pond there are a few things that they need to keep them as stress-free and healthy as possible: plenty of plant cover, enough oxygen, the correct amount of food and sufficient space. A healthy pond will also attract other wildlife – amphibians such as frogs and perhaps insects such as dragonflies.

Aeration and shade

Even if your pond usually has ample oxygen for the fish, during a heatwave prompt action may be needed. Warm water absorbs oxygen from the surface less efficiently than cold water, and depleted oxygen in a small water feature is the most common cause of fish distress. Without the cooler, deeper water and shade from surface leaves to shelter under, fish will be gulping for oxygen at the surface in hot weather. Supply extra oxygen by spraying the water surface or installing a small air block, which pumps bubbling air into the water.

Feeding

More damage to the pool chemistry is caused by overfeeding fish than any other practice. Uneaten food gradually sinks to the bottom and decomposes, causing a build-up of unwanted decaying matter. Although fish in a small pool become dependent on your feeding, this is generally overdone. The fish should devour their meal in five to ten minutes. If you use floating food, you can see what is left after this period and remove it and then adjust the amount of food you give them at ensuing meals.

Fish in a small pool are more likely to have an unnatural diet of dried food, and supplements will be a welcome and valuable treat. Live food, such as daphnia, which is sold in large fish retailers, is ideal, and if this is not available freeze-dried and frozen foods are a good second best.

Providing ample plant life is the best answer, because fish forage for all sorts of eggs and larvae of other creatures to obtain a balanced diet. The water temperature should be watched carefully in spring and autumn, because feeding when the water is too cold results in undigested food remaining in the gut of the fish. When the temperature falls towards 10°C (50°F) feed them on wheat germ flakes or pellets, which can be digested more easily than other types of food. Stop feeding them completely when the temperature drops below this level.

Right and below right To reduce the shock of a rapid temperature change, leave the fish in the bag to float for an hour or two before gently introducing the pond water and releasing the fish.

Pests and diseases

As long as the fish are not over-crowded, they should be relatively disease free, especially if they were bought from a reliable source and were healthy when introduced to the pool. There are, nevertheless, one or two problems to look out for, the most common of which is predation by herons. The fact that the pool is near the house or in a relatively built-up area will not prevent a heron from taking an interest in your fish. Late spring and autumn are the two most common times for attack. Once a heron has found and taken fish from your pool, it becomes a persistent visitor as long as there are fish to take.

Numerous devices are sold to deter herons, of which the least effective is the decoy heron, seen gracing the sides of many a domestic pool. The most effective system uses a thin line, similar to fishing line, held under slight tension about 30–45cm (12–18in) above the ground and around the pool. When the heron lands a little distance away from the pool and walks to the pool side, it catches the wire and releases the tension, which sets off a small toy cap gun. This frightens the heron, and after a couple of times is usually enough to stop the visits. Inconspicuous fishing wire, whether connected to a device or not, is by far the most successful deterrent, and serious fish-keepers often almost totally enclose their pools in pergola-like structures over which fishing lines are strung at regular intervals.

There are numerous other creatures that live in the pool that are regarded as fish pests, but these tend only to attack fish fry or very small fish. Once a fish is 5–8cm (2–3in) long it is reasonably safe from attack from creatures like the great diving beetle, water scorpions and dragonfly larvae.

Size will not prevent disease from attacking on occasions, and this will be more likely in an unbalanced pool that is heavily polluted or lacking in ade-

quate oxygen. Overstocking also makes fish more susceptible to disease, especially when there is inadequate food or only an unbalanced diet available. The most common diseases under these poor environmental conditions are fungus disease or 'cotton wool' disease, and 'white spot'; both are sure signs of weak fish unable to fight infection in a wound to a scale or an attack by a parasite.

Other wildlife

Small features with open water will soon attract other forms of wildlife that seem to appear from nowhere. Many of these are extremely beneficial to the garden – toads and frogs will help in the battle against slugs and snails. Even if you do not deliberately introduce spawn, these amphibians seem to have an uncanny knack of finding water no matter how small the

area, and the most important thing is to not trap them inside the pools by having vertical sides with a gap between the surround and the water level. The stems of marginal plants will help them clamber out, as will cobbles and small ramps of wood from the top of a marginal aquatic container. Rather than cutting back the stems of marginal plants in autumn, as you would in a formal pool, leave them until spring. They will provide welcome winter protection for a host of small creatures.

Visitors will not be restricted to the amphibians. If there are shallow edges, birds will soon learn to use them for bathing and drinking, and don't be surprised to see more insects, like dragonflies, looking for a place to lay eggs. Having some native plants in the planting scheme adds to the attraction as the food supply is more available for insects in native flowers.

Left A wide sheet of flexible liner was used to give this wildlife stream damp soil edging to provide an attractive home for newts, frogs and toads in the dense cover.

Aquatic plants have two roles – they keep the water clear and enhance the water feature through the beauty of foliage and flowers. Your planting scheme should balance both these functions using various types of aquatic plant, from inconspicuous submerged plants to the more showy marginal plants.

PLANTS AND PLANTING TECHNIQUES

AQUATIC PLANTS

Aquatic plants are divided into four main categories: oxygenators, floaters, deep-water plants and marginals. Sometimes garden and aquatic centres have displays of a fifth category, known as moisture-lovers or bog plants, but these will also grow in normal soil provided it is damp, and they are not, therefore, regarded as true aquatics.

Right Even in this tiny cascading stream, the full range of aquatic plants is represented, from the milfoil peeping above the surface to the moisture-lovers on the banks.

during daylight hours, and this is highly beneficial to water chemistry and fish.

Oxygenators are leafy, soft plants with small roots; they depend on their leaves for the absorption of nutrients dissolved in pool water. These are also required by algae. and in the competition for the food, the oxygenators generally win and gradually starve out the algae. Oxygenators also provide homes for fish fry and other animal life and help these creatures survive the cannabalistic tendencies of adult fish.

A small water feature like a trough or sink has such a low water volume that one oxygenating plant will probably be enough, because they grow quickly and soon need cutting back. For larger pools the quantity required can be roughly calculated by referring to the surface area of the pool. The oxygenators are sold as bunches of unrooted stem cuttings, and it is usually recommended that five bunches be added for every 1 sq m (10 sq ft) of surface area. Five or six main species of oxygenating plant are normally sold, and it is best to mix the species rather than buy just one type.

Floating plants

As the name suggests, this group of aquatics floats on the surface. They have no anchorage on the bottom and their roots dangle in the water, obtaining the nutrients they need from this surface layer of water. They also help to keep down algae by competing for dissolved mineral salts and shading out light, which algae need. They quickly spread in a pool and will require netting off if they cover the surface.

Oxygenating plants

The oxygenators or submerged plants are the most important group for small water features because of their role in keeping down algae. Even if you do not have room for some of the other larger plants such as marginals, you must include some oxygenators in your small pool. These submerged plants thrive in water 60–90cm (2–3ft) deep. In deeper water there is insufficient light for them to survive.

They are called oxygenating plants because of their role in supplying oxygen

Eichhornia crassipes (water hyacinth) and *Pistia stratiotes* (water lettuce) are not hardy and are only available in late spring when the water warms up and all danger of frost has passed. They can be overwintered on mud in shallow trays in a light, frost-free place. The most efficient are *Lemna* spp. (duckweed), which come into growth in early spring before waterlily leaves surface. This is when the water has least shade and is vulnerable to greening up in strong spring sunshine.

Deep-water plants

The waterlilies dominate this group of aquatics, which have their roots in the deeper water of the pool and develop leaves on the surface. Apart from their flowers' decorative value, the leaves are vital in high summer in shading the pool and maintaining water clarity. There are species and cultivars suitable for varying depths of water, from 20cm (8in) to 60cm (2ft) above the crown. Aim to cover between half and two-thirds of the water surface with leaves; the spread of each plant (see pages 144–8) will help you decide how many to plant.

Marginals

These plants grow around the margins of a pool, in anything from mud to 23cm (9in) of water. There is a greater variety of plants in this group of aquatics than the others, and their main role is decorative. In a small wildlife pool they provide cover for waterfowl and other visiting creatures. Many form large clumps in their natural surroundings, but can be grown in smaller pools if they are kept to a manageable size by restricting their roots in planting containers. Marginal shelves of preformed pools are designed for these plants, which sit on the shelves in flat-bottomed aquatic baskets.

Moisture-loving plants

These are plants that grow in the moist soil near pools and streams but must

Left Two reliable marginals, *Iris laevigata* en masse and the bushier *Mimulus* 'Wisley Red' in the foreground.

not have their roots waterlogged for any length of time. They are not strictly aquatic plants but make lovely associations with water. They need their roots permanently moist to reach their full potential, and common examples are primulas, hostas and astilbes.

Moisture-loving plants, such as *Cornus* spp. (dogwood) and *Salix* spp. (willow), are often grown around wildlife pools, where they provide cover for wildlife, but also have colourful winter stems. In spring these plants should be cut back to within a few inches of the ground. This will encourage bushy and

more colourful shoots for next winter. Fork over the bed after pruning and apply an organic mulch to retain the winter's moisture in the soil.

In autumn, as slightly tender moisture-loving plants die down and the leaves turn brown, the large leaves of plants like *Gunnera manicata* can be cut off and placed over the crown of the plant to protect it in winter. In addition to the plants' own leaves, falling leaves from trees or leaf mould can also be used over the crowns and covered with wire mesh so that they are not blown off by winter winds.

PLANTING TECHNIQUES

In a small water feature aquatic plants are best planted in plastic aquatic containers, which differ from pots and planters for normal soil in having permeable mesh sides and wide, flat bases to give extra stability under the water. The mesh sides enable water and gases to move easily in and out of the compost in the container.

Above Waterlilies are increasingly sold in containers with a convenient handle to help lower them into the water.

Aquatic baskets are available in a range of sizes and shapes and are of two main types: those with wide mesh and those with fine, louvre-type mesh. Those with wide mesh have to be lined with a permeable material, such as hessian or woven polypropylene, which allows gases and water to move in and out but stops compost seeping out. The fine, louvre-type mesh types require no lining. For very small barrels or troughs use the smallest containers to allow a variety of planting.

In addition to traditional containers, there are non-rigid, bag-type ones with floats so you do not need a marginal shelf, and cubes of rockwool, in which the plant is already growing, that can simply be dropped into the pool.

Compost

Aquatic plant compost is not the same as that used for terrestrial plants, even though many composts are marked 'multi-purpose'. As they will become completely saturated there is no need for moisture-retaining ingredients like peat, or drainage materials like sharp sand. This leaves the prime ingredient for aquatic plants as loam, and proprietary aquatic composts sold in bags are simply that. You may already have masses of this in your garden, particularly if you have stripped off any turf and stacked it to rot for a few months. Good topsoil can also be used if it is a heavy loam and has not had any chemicals applied in recent months.

Planting time

Unlike shrubs and herbaceous plants, which are generally planted when they are dormant in winter or early spring, aquatic plants should be in full growth when they are planted, and the ideal time is late spring or early summer. Stop planting after late summer because the young plants will not have had enough time to begin growing before they become dormant

Planting depth

Different waterlilies should be planted at different depths, and this should be indicated on the plant label. This variation also applies to the marginals and if the label has no information, the plant in question may be among the key plants included on pages 138–51, where the appropriate planting depth is indicated. Remember that the rec-ommended depth refers to the depth of water above the growing point or crown of the plant and not the base of the planting container.

Oxygenators

Fill the container to the brim with loamy soil, then firm it thoroughly so that there is a gap of 2.5–5cm (1–2in) from the top of the container to the firmed compost. Use a dibber to make a hole about 8cm (3in) deep in each corner and one in the centre. Insert the bunch of oxygenators so that the clasp holding them together is buried under the surface of the compost. Firm around the planted bunch then top-dress the compost with a 2.5cm (1in) layer of pea shingle. This prevents particles of dry compost floating when the plants are immersed in water. Place the container on the bottom of the pool. For sinks and barrels use a small aquatic pots about 8cm (3in) across to plant a single oxygenator; this will be sufficient for such a small space.

Floaters

Tip floating plants on to the water surface if they are the small-leaved plants like *Lemna* spp. (duckweed) or *Azolla filiculoides* (fairy moss). Larger plants, such as *Eichhornia crassipes* (water hyacinth), may have lost some of their buoyancy if they have been in bags for some time, so lift them gently on to a corner of the pool where they are not blown about until they grow upright again. It really doesn't matter where the floaters are placed on the pool surface: the wind will blow them about.

Practicalities

Sowing seed

Seed can be collected to increase stock from plants that are difficult to divide, such as *Orontium aquaticum* (golden club). Seed from aquatic plants is best sown fresh into small seed pans, which are then placed in a washing-up bowl. For deep-water plants, like *Orontium aquaticum* or *Aponogeton distachyos* (water hawthorn), the water should just cover the seed pan. For marginals or moisture-lovers, like primulas, the water should be just under the seed pan. Seedheads that are not required for propagation should be removed.

PLANTING A POND

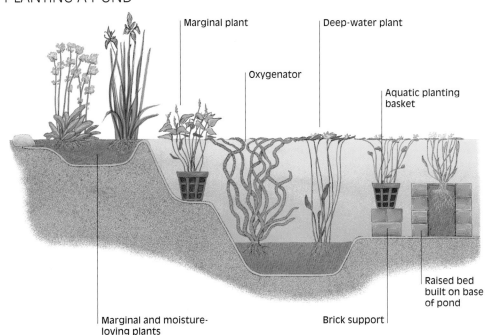

Marginal plant
Deep-water plant
Oxygenator
Aquatic planting basket
Marginal and moisture-loving plants
Brick support
Raised bed built on base of pond

Deep-water plants

These are most likely to be waterlilies so the procedure described is appropriate for this group of plants. Other deep-water plants are treated in the same way except that they are always planted vertically, whereas some waterlilies are planted at an angle in the compost.

There are two types of waterlily: tuberous rooted and rhizome rooted. The roots of the tuberous-rooted waterlilies resemble pineapples; these are planted upright. The other type, the rhizome-rooted waterlilies, which are the majority, will have a flat-growing root with the growing point slightly angled upwards at the tip. This type is planted with the root almost horizontal just under the compost.

When you buy young plants, if they are not already growing in a container, you will see a small piece of the root at the growing tip and this may be too small for you to be able to identify the type. There is no need to worry whether a piece of root of this size is planted at an angle or not; the root shape of the older roots is the only reliable guide, and this will be apparent on larger pieces of root.

The vigour or spread of the plant will suggest the suitable size of container, but in a small water feature, where you are likely to want a miniature waterlily, you will need only a small container. Firm the compost well into the container and push the root just under the surface with the growing point sticking out. Top-dress the compost with pea shingle and place in shallow water initially until the leaves are growing strongly. If there is no shallow shelf in the pool to start the plant, build a temporary pier of bricks on the bottom so that the plant is only 15cm (6in) under the surface. As the leaves gain strength and are in full growth, remove the bricks one at a time until the plant can rest on the bottom.

Marginals

Marginals should be planted in medium to large size containers. Fill the container with aquatic compost and firm thoroughly. Plant the young marginal to the same depth in the compost that it was growing before and firm in thoroughly. Top-dress the compost with pea shingle and place the container on the marginal shelf.

Left A young containerized waterlily positioned in the shallower water until it matures in a few months when it can be moved to the deeper water in the centre.

CARE AND MAINTENANCE

Add plants or fish to a water feature and, unlike the closed recirculating systems like cobble fountains and brimming urns, some care and attention will be required. Aquatic plants grow very quickly and soon become overgrown even in relatively small containers. Much of the care will relate to curtailing this lush growth by cutting it back and dividing the plants frequently.

Top Thicker iris roots can be divided by cutting through them with a knife and retaining the outer portions.

Above After planting the divided portions, cut back the leaves and top dress the new compost with pea shingle.

Feeding

In a small pool there should be no need to add fertilizer to the planting compost because it could dissolve quickly and cloud the water by feeding the algae with mineral salts. For large waterlilies in a large lake the planting compost should have nutrients added, but in small volumes of water, wait for at least a year before adding a slow-release fertilizer in the form of a sachet pushed into the container. Only feed with this type of sachet; unlike ordinary fertilizer, it won't dissolve rapidly in the water causing algae to grow.

The oxygenators will get all the nutrients they need from the water, and the only group likely to become starved quickly are the vigorous forms of the marginals as they are restricted in containers. Rather than feed these *in situ*, it is better to lift out the marginals every year, divide them and plant them into fresh compost. This prevents them from looking starved in the centre of the plant with all the young, healthy growth on the outside of the crown.

Pruning

In no time the freshly planted pool will be full of growth, and if there is only a small container, pruning will soon be necessary, particularly of the oxygenators. If this is not done regularly, all the soft sappy growth dies down in winter, polluting and de-oxygenating the water. Pruning is easy: simply nip the growth off near the base, leaving short stems. The young growth can be used as cuttings if you need them, but the cut stems will soon regrow. The best time to do this is mid- to late summer.

It will be some time before the waterlilies need pruning: they generally indicate this by thrusting their leaves above the water surface and stopping flowering. Lift the plants out of the water and cut off the young growth about 8–10cm (3–4in) long behind the growing tip, discarding the older pieces and leaves. The young tip is replanted as described on page 137. Waterlilies constantly replace their leaves and as part of regular pool maintenance the older yellowing leaves should be cut off.

When marginal plants start growth in spring, the fresh green leaves appear among any old brown foliage. These old leaves should be removed in spring but be careful not to cut across all the leaves as if you were trimming grass or a hedge with shears as you may cut the tips of the young leaves. Use secateurs to remove dry and fibrous old foliage.

Pests

All plants are subject to some forms of pest or disease, and aquatic plants are no exception, although most of the

Practicalities

Dividing and repotting

If you need to clean out the pool, take the opportunity to divide and repot before replanting. Only the young tips of the waterlilies will need replanting and their containers should be propped up on temporary brick piers to support the plants near the surface until the leaves are growing strongly again. Cuttings can be taken of the oxygenators: take pieces about 23cm (9in) long, bunch them together and plant in their original containers in fresh aquatic compost. Marginals should be divided with a spade or fork and the young outer growth replanted in the same container in fresh aquatic compost or garden loam. Dividing floaters is also necessary but is a much simpler process – simply net off older plants regularly.

problems are disfiguring rather than lethal. Controlling pests and diseases by chemicals is more difficult if there are fish in the pool, because the slightest whiff of insecticide near water will affect fish. Biological control should be practised as much as possible, and here fish are very useful. Most insect infestations occur above the level at which fish can reach them.Direct a strong jet of water on to the foliage above the water level to dislodge the pests, which will be devoured by the fish. If chemicals are used, it is best to remove the plant first and immerse it in a bucket or large container full of the diluted insecticide. After being submerged for an hour or two, the plant should be thoroughly rinsed before being returned to the pool.

Because waterlilies are among the most decorative plants in the pool, pests or diseases are easily noticed. Problems are mainly confined to the leaves, where boring, biting and tunnelling larvae cause severe disfigurement if not caught early.

The most common offenders that weaken rather than seriously disfigure are greenfly and leafhoppers, both of which suck sap from young growth just above water level. Leaves flat on the surface are more easily reached by fish to control them, but where waterlilies are overgrown and hold their leaves well above the water, infestations become severe, causing the leaves to go brown.

Less common but more disfiguring are the larval stages of certain beetles, midges, moths and flies. Caddis fly larvae, for instance, swim about with protective cases around their bodies spun from fragments of leaves, sticks, sand and pieces of shell. They feed on young waterlily leaves, completely devouring them in severe attacks. It is impossible to control chemically; you have to rely on their natural enemies of carp, goldfish and orfe to keep them under control. This method of larvae protecting themselves in cases of vegetation is also used by the caterpillars of a small moth,

about 2.5cm (1in) long, often seen at dusk over the water. After the caterpillars hatch they shred leaves to form the cases, then proceed to eat large holes in the waterlily pads, sometimes skeletonizing the leaves completely.

Possibly the greatest disfigurement of leaves is caused by larvae of the leaf-mining midge, which, after hatching from eggs laid on the leaf surface, burrow just under it, causing raised serpentine channels in the skin. The most destructive pests are waterlily beetle grubs. This small beetle makes up for its size of 6mm (¼in) by laying clusters of eggs on the leaves in summer. The eggs hatch into tiny black larvae with yellow bellies that devastate the leaves by eating the tissue between the veins. These larvae pupate on foliage above the waterline in autumn, and where attacks are severe, the biological control is to remove any aerial foliage in autumn.

Diseases

Only a few diseases disfigure aquatic plants, mainly fungal leaf spot. One attacks waterlilies, causing spots on the leaves: these sometimes extend to dark patches and dry, brown edges. Removing infected leaves by hand is the only cure except spraying with fungicides. Irises also get a leaf spot that sometimes elongates from random brown spots to brown streaks in the direction of the veins. If the leaves are far enough away from the water to prevent drift, a wide-spectrum fungicide, such as dithiocarbamate, can be used early in the infection.

Occasionally waterlilies get a lethal rot that affects the crowns. It begins with the leaves yellowing and the leaf stems turning brown and rotting. The whole plant looks extremely sick, and if it is removed from the water the root appears soft and gelatinous with the most vile smell. There is no cure and infected plants should be destroyed.

Perhaps the most common disease seen is mildew, particularly on some calthas. Cut the foliage away completely: the plant will regrow rapidly, often without mildew.

Water snails are common in most pools, and where there is ample vegetation their damage is hardly noticeable. In a barrel or trough they could be more of a problem and can be trapped by floating a lettuce leaf on the surface. The following morning the snails will be found under the lettuce leaf.

Above A colourful array of moisture-loving plants which are taking advantage of the extra moisture which wicks up from the pool in just the right quantity.

OXYGENATING PLANTS

A selection of oxygenating plants should be planted in the deeper water and cut back regularly because they soon become straggly. They are not planted for their ornamental value but for their role in producing and maintaining clear water. A smaller feature will require no more than one or two plants, but in an open pool with a minimum size of 2 sq m (21½ sq ft) it would be sensible to mix the species.

Callitriche hermaphroditica (syn. C. autumnalis)
Autumnal starwort

A submerged perennial with thin, branching stems to 50cm (20in) long and small, narrow, light green leaves, 3cm (1¼in) long and 1mm (⅟₂in) wide. It is an excellent oxygenator and also a refuge for freshwater fleas, shrimps and fish fry, which need good supplies of oxygen. Unlike most starworts, it does not develop surface rosettes and grows mainly near pool bottoms.

- **Spread** indefinite
- **Water depth** to 50cm (20in)
- Hardy
- Full sun
- **Propagation** stem cuttings in spring or summer

Fontinalis antipyretica
Water moss, willow moss

An evergreen perennial moss with round or triangular, branched stems, 20–25cm (8–20in) long, and olive green, moss-like leaves, 5cm (2in) long by 4cm (1½in) wide, which grow directly from the stem and overlap each other like scales. Grow in full light in shallow water, weighting the plants on to boulders, where they form a dense carpet, which acts as a good oxygenator. Excellent in moving water.

- **Height** 8cm (3in)
- **Spread** indefinite
- **Water depth** 45cm (18in)
- Hardy
- Sun or shade
- **Propagation** bunched cuttings

Hottonia palustris
Water violet

An attractive perennial oxygenator, bearing both decorative foliage and aerial flowers. It produces stolons and erect stems, which bear whorls of deeply divided, light green leaves, 2–13cm (¾–5in) long and 6–10mm (¼–⅟₂in) wide. Erect spikes, 30–40cm (12–16in) long, emerge above the water in spring, bearing pale lilac flowers, 2–2.5cm (¾–1in) across. They are not easy to establish and perform best in shallow, clear, mud-bottomed pools rather than in planting baskets.

- **Height** 30–90cm (1–3ft)
- **Spread** indefinite
- **Water depth** to 45cm (18in)
- Hardy
- Sun or shade
- **Propagation** stem cuttings in spring or summer

Ceratophyllum demersum
Hornwort

A perennial with slender, often rootless stems growing to 30–60cm (1–2ft) long, supporting whorls of brittle, dark green, forked leaves, 1–4cm (½–1½in) long, which become denser near the growing point. It is tolerant of shade and will grow in deeper water than most submerged aquatics. It tolerates a wide range of water conditions and makes an excellent oxygenator and a refuge for fish fry.

- **Spread** indefinite
- **Water depth** to 60cm (2ft)
- Hardy
- Sun or shade
- **Propagation** stem cuttings in spring or early summer

Ceratophyllum demersum

Lagarosiphon major (syn. Elodea crispa)

A semi-evergreen perennial with branched, fragile stems to 1m (3ft) long covered in curling leaves, 6–25mm (¼–1in) long and 2–3mm (¹⁄₁₆–⅛in) wide. Used extensively as an oxygenator, it forms dense, submerged masses of branched stems, which should be cut back every autumn.

- **Spread** indefinite
- **Water depth** 90cm (3ft)
- **Hardy**
- **Full sun**
- **Propagation** cuttings at any time in growing season

Myriophyllum aquaticum (syn. M. brasiliense, M. proserpinacoides)
Milfoil, parrot's feather, diamond milfoil

A perennial with spreading stems, 90cm (1m) long, and tightly packed, needle-like, bright green leaves, borne in whorls. The inconspicuous yellowish flowers are borne on a spike to 15cm (6in) tall just above the water surface in summer. The delicate leaves create excellent homes for fish fry as well as oxygenating the water. Often amphibious, it makes a good subject for softening shallow edges and for scrambling over the sides of troughs or barrels. It needs a minimum water temperature of 1°C (34°F).

- **Spread** indefinite
- **Water depth** 45cm (18in)
- **Half-hardy**
- **Sun or shade**
- **Propagation** cuttings in spring or summer

Potamogeton crispus
Curled pondweed

A perennial with long, cylindrical stems, bearing narrow, almost translucent leaves, 10cm (4in) long and 3–15mm (⅛–⅝in) wide, with wavy edges when mature. The small, crimson and creamy white flowers emerge just above the water surface in summer. The leaves provide a home for fish fry, and plants spread rapidly in mud-bottomed pools and will tolerate cloudy or shady water better than any other oxygenator.

- **Height** indefinite
- **Spread** indefinite
- **Water depth** 90cm (3ft)
- **Hardy**
- **Sun or shade**
- **Propagation** stem cuttings in spring or early summer

Myriophyllum aquaticum

Ranunculus aquatilis

Ranunculus aquatilis
Water crowfoot

An annual or perennial with deeply lobed, kidney-shaped, floating leaves, 3–8cm (1¼–3in) long. The buttercup-shaped, white flowers, which are held above the water, are 2cm (¾in) across with a yellow base to the petals. They are best at a depth of 15–60cm (6–24in), when they can root in a mud bottom.

- **Height** indefinite
- **Spread** indefinite
- **Water depth** 90cm (3ft)
- **Hardy**
- **Sun or shade**
- **Propagation** seed or division in spring or summer

FLOATING PLANTS

These useful and decorative free-floating species require no more than scattering on the surface of the water. They are valuable in the initial stages of establishing a pool when they provide much needed shade. In the right conditions, all these floating plants have an indefinite spread and require no more than netting off when they outgrow their space.

Azolla filiculoides

Azolla filiculoides (syn. *A. caroliniana*)
Fairy moss, water fern, mosquito fern

This small perennial fern forms clusters of soft, pale green leaves, which turn purplish-red in autumn. Each leaf is attached to a single fine root. It can be invasive, so thin regularly. It is slightly tender but can be overwintered on mud in a frost-free place.

- **Spread** indefinite
- **Half-hardy**
- **Full sun**
- **Propagation** division

Eichhornia crassipes (syn. *E. speciosa*)
Water hyacinth

An attractive evergreen or semi-evergreen floater, which forms clumps of buoyant foliage on spongy, swollen stalks. In warm summers it produces pale blue, hyacinth-like flowers, to 15–23cm (6–9in high). It may root in any mud in shallow water but needs a sheltered position.

- **Height** 23–30cm (9–12in)
- **Spread** indefinite
- **Tender**
- **Full sun**
- **Propagation** division in spring or summer

Pistia stratiotes

Lemna trisulca
Ivy-leaved duckweed

Most of the duckweeds are too rampant for small pools, but this species is not quite as vigorous as most and can be netted off when it gets out of hand. The light green leaves are just below the water surface, except at flowering time, and are about 1cm (½in) across, each with a single rootlet.

- **Spread** indefinite
- **Hardy**
- **Sun or shade**
- **Propagation** division

Pistia stratiotes
Water lettuce, shell flower
A deciduous floating aquatic, which is evergreen in warm climates where the minimum temperature is no less than 10°C (50°F). The overlapping, pale green leaves, which resemble a lettuce in their arrangement, are velvety and whitish-green on the undersides. Keep thinning new plants in summer.

- **Height** 23–30cm (9–12in)
- **Spread** indefinite
- **Water depth** to 90cm (3ft)
- **Tender**
- **Sun**
- **Propagation** separate plantlets

Salvinia auriculata
Butterfly fern
A floating fern, which is evergreen in warm climates where the minimum temperature falls no lower than 10°C (50°F). The pale green or purplish-brown leaves, which are covered in silky hairs, are tightly arranged on branched stems.

- Height 2.5cm (1in)

- **Spread** indefinite
- **Tender**
- **Full sun**
- **Propagation** separate stems

Stratiotes aloides
Water soldier
A semi-evergreen, perennial floater that forms prickly rosettes of olive green leaves, 50cm (20in) long and 2.5cm (1in) wide, with serrated edges. The tips of the leaves frequently emerge above the water surface. In summer the plant tries to surface to produce cup-shaped, white, sometimes pink-tinged flowers, about 4cm (1¾in) across.

- **Height** 40cm (16in)
- **Spread** indefinite
- **Water depth** to 90cm (3ft)
- **Hardy**
- **Sun**
- **Propagation** remove offsets

Lemna trisulca

Eichhornia crassipes

DEEP-WATER PLANTS

In addition to the waterlily, which dominates this group of plants, there is a small selection of plants that produce floating leaves but have their root systems in deeper water. In addition to their ornamental value, the surface leaves help to shade out the algae. They make a good alternative to waterlilies where there is insufficient sun for the waterlilies to flower. A selection of waterlilies is included on pages 145–48.

Aponogeton distachyos

Aponogeton distachyos
Water hawthorn, Cape pondweed

This perennial has oblong, bright green leaves, to 20cm (8in) long by 8cm (3in) wide, which can be almost evergreen in mild winters. The strongly scented flowers, 10cm (4in) long, are often produced in two flushes, spring and autumn, and are white with purple-brown anthers. They are held above the surface. A tolerant plant, this extends the flowering season on the water surface and provides a change to the circular pads of waterlilies.

- **Spread** 1.2m (4ft)
- **Water depth** 60cm (2ft)
- Frost hardy
- Sun or shade
- **Propagation** seed or division in spring

Hydrocharis morsus-ranae
Frogbit

A perennial with runners that form new plants with rosettes of kidney-shaped, shiny green leaves, 2.5cm (1in) across. The papery white flowers, 2cm (⅜in) across, have three petals with a yellow centre. They form a home and shade for colonies of life in shallow warm areas of wildlife pools where roots can form in mud. They are rather vulnerable to snail damage.

- **Spread** Indefinite
- **Water depth** to 30cm (12in)
- Hardy
- Full sun
- **Propagation** remove plantlets

Nuphar japonica
Japanese pond lily

This perennial has narrow, oval surface leaves, 40cm (16in) long and 12cm (5in) wide, and submerged, wavy, heart-shaped leaves, 30cm (12in) long and to 12cm (5in) wide. The round, yellow flowers, held just above the surface in summer, are 5cm (2in) across. Although more tolerant of deeper water and shade than most waterlilies, the Japanese pond lily requires more sun for optimum flower production than its more vigorous relatives *Nuphar advena* (American spatterdock) and *N. lutea* (common pond lily).

- **Spread** 90cm (3ft)
- **Water depth** 30cm (12in)
- Hardy
- Full sun
- **Propagation** division in spring

Orontium aquaticum
Golden club

A deciduous perennial, with bluish-green leaves, with a silvery sheen on the underside, which float in deep water. The poker-like yellow flowerheads on white stalks stand well above the water.

- **Height** 30–45cm (12–18in)
- **Spread** 60cm (2ft)
- **Water depth** 30cm (1ft)
- Hardy
- Full sun
- **Propagation** seed or division in spring

Persicaria amphibia
Willow grass, amphibious bistort

An amphibious perennial with long-stalked floating leaves, 8–10cm (3–4in) long and 2–4cm (¾–1¾in) wide, borne on stems 30–90cm (1–3ft) long, which root from the stems. The densely packed pink flowers are borne on spikes 5cm (2in) above the water in midsummer. A useful and attractive plant for shallow margins of informal pools.

- **Spread** indefinite
- **Water depth** to 45cm (18in)
- Hardy
- Full sun
- **Propagation** seed or division in early spring

Orontium aquaticum

WATERLILIES

The waterlilies (*Nymphaea* species and cultivars) described here are the medium and small spreading types; the vigorous waterlilies that need large pools and lakes are not included. While the majority are hardy, the selection includes some tender waterlilies, which in temperate areas need to be lifted in winter and kept in a frost-free place, such as a greenhouse or conservatory where there is ample light.

The spread refers to the average area that the leaves will cover when planted in a large planting crate. In small planting crates they will not achieve these dimensions, but if the roots escape from the containers and root into bottom mud, the dimensions may be exceeded. The planting depth specified refers to the depth of water above the growing point, not the depth of the pool, and the depth given is for mature plants that have been established some time with ample root systems. If in doubt, it is always better to plant a waterlily in shallower than deeper water It is assumed that they all require the sunniest position possible. The cultivars described here can be propagated by division; species can be grown from seed.

Nymphaea 'Blue Beauty'

Nymphaea 'Aurora'
A free-flowering waterlily bearing changeable, slightly scented, cup-shaped, later star-shaped, day-blooming, semi-double flowers, 5cm (2in) across. It has the widest colour range in its flower of any changeable cultivar. The flowers are cream in bud, opening to yellow, then passing through orange to a slightly flecked blood red with glowing golden-orange stamens. The olive green leaves, 15–16.5cm (6–6½in) across, have several small, red-purple blotches.

- **Spread** 75cm (30in)
- **Planting depth** 30–45cm (12–18in)
- Hardy

Nymphaea 'Blue Beauty'
The day-blooming, star-shaped, very sweetly scented flowers are 20–28cm (8–11in) across, with rich blue petals and deep yellow stamens. The excellent colour and prolific blooming make this a highly recommended cultivar, which should be planted only when the weather has turned warm in spring. It has wavy-edged leaves, 33–35cm (13–14in) across, slightly speckled with purple blotches and with purple-brown undersides.

- **Spread** 90cm (3ft)
- **Planting depth** 30–45cm (12–18in)
- Tender

Nymphaea candida
The white, cup-shaped flowers, 8cm (3in) across, are held above the water. They have white petals and sepals tinged with green. The light green leaves are round and 15cm (6in) across. It is well worth growing in a small tub or pool in cooler areas.

- **Spread** 30–60cm (1–2ft)
- **Planting depth** 15–30cm (6–12in)
- Hardy

Nymphaea capensis
Cape blue waterlily
The day-blooming, star-shaped, light blue flowers with deep yellow stamens are 23–25cm (9–10in) across and held above the water. The leaves, 25–40cm (10–16in) across, are almost round, dentate and wavy edged. This is an adaptable species, which will grow in all sizes of pool.

- **Spread** 1–2m (3–6ft)
- **Planting depth** 30cm (12in)
- Tender

Practicalities

Oily deposits on the water
As waterlily leaves decay on the surface they tend to leave a thin film of streaky oil on the surface. Removing the leaves as soon as they go yellow is the best solution, but if this has not been possible and you notice the oily film, place large sheets of newspaper on the surface. The paper will absorb the oil and any other debris, like dust and pollen, which is too light to sink.

Nymphaea 'Escarboucle'

medium-sized pool. It stays open later in the afternoon than most other hardy reds.

- **Spread** 1.2–1.5m (4–5ft)
- **Planting depth** 30–60cm (1–2ft)
- Hardy

Nymphaea 'Firecrest'

The star-shaped, lavender-pink flowers, which are held slightly above the water, are 15cm (6in) across, with orange inner stamens and pink outer stamens. Dark purple young leaves mature to round green leaves, 23cm (9in) across. It needs a container 60cm (2ft) across by 30cm (1ft) deep so that the rhizomes can develop.

- **Spread** 1.2m (4ft)
- **Planting depth** 30–45cm (12–18in)
- Hardy

Nymphaea 'Froebelii'

The cup-shaped, burgundy red flowers become star-shaped, 10–12cm (4–5in) across, with orange-red stamens. Bronzed young leaves mature to round, pale green leaves, 15cm (6in) across. This is a good cultivar for cooler climates and a very good waterlily for barrels or small pools.

- **Spread** 90cm (3ft)
- **Planting depth** 15–30cm (6–12in)
- *Hardy*

Nymphaea 'Gonnère'

The globe-shaped, fragrant, day-blooming, white flowers, 10–15cm (4–6in) across, have yellow stamens. Slightly bronzed young leaves mature to round, green leaves, 15–23cm (6–9in) across. Ideal for all sized pools, this magnificent snowball-white flower stays open late in the day.

- **Spread** 0.9–1.2m (3–4ft)
- **Planting depth** 30–45cm (12–18in)
- Hardy

Nymphaea 'Ellisiana'

The star-shaped, red flowers, about 9cm (3.5in) across, intensify in colour from pinkish-mauve to red, with the centre petals sitting upright while the sepals remain flat. The flowers are further enhanced by the yellow stamens emerging from the purple bases of the petals. The young leaves are dark green with purple blotches, maturing to almost round, 18–20cm (7–8in) across. This is an ideal cultivar for small tubs and troughs and performs particularly well in cooler regions, tending to stop flowering when the weather gets very hot.

- **Spread** 30–60cm (1–2ft)
- **Planting depth** 15–23cm (6–9in)
- Hardy

Nymphaea 'Escarboucle'

The cup-shaped flowers become star-shaped, about 15–17cm (6–7in) across. They are bright vermilion red with the outer petals tipped white and deep orange stamens. Brown-tinged young leaves mature to round, green leaves, 25–27cm (10–11in) across. This is one of the best red hardy waterlilies for a

Nymphaea 'James Brydon'

The cup-shaped, brilliant rose-red, day-blooming flowers, 10–12cm (4–5in) across, have orange-red stamens. Purplish-brown young leaves, blotched with dark purple, mature to round green leaves, 17cm (7in) across. This is a popular cultivar for barrels or medium-sized pools. It is one of the finest red waterlilies and is resistant to crown rot.

- **Spread** 0.9–1.2m (3–4ft)
- **Planting depth** 30–45cm (12–18in)
- Hardy

Nymphaea 'Laydekeri Fulgens'

The cup-shaped, burgundy red, day-blooming flowers are 12–15cm (5–6in) across and have orange-red stamens. Purplish-green young leaves, blotched with dark purple, mature to round green leaves, 21cm (8in) across. One of the first to bloom in spring, this magnificent cultivar is free flowering throughout summer and is suitable for all sized pools.

- **Planting depth** 30–45cm (12–18in)
- **Spread** 1.2–1.5m (4–5ft)
- Hardy

Nymphaea 'Lucida'

The star-shaped, day-blooming flowers, 12–15cm (5–6in) across, have red inner petals and whitish-pink outer petals with pink veins and yellow stamens. The broadly ovate, mature leaves, speckled with large purple blotches, grow to 25cm (10in) long and 23cm (9in) wide. A free-flowering cultivar with most attractive leaves, this is suitable for any sized pool.

- **Planting depth** 30–45cm (12–18in)
- **Spread** 1.2–1.5m (4–5ft)
- Hardy

Nymphaea 'Marliacea Albida'

The cup-shaped, day-blooming, white flowers, 12–15cm (5–6in) across, have yellow stamens. Slightly bronzed young leaves mature to round green leaves, 23cm (9in) across. This free-flowering cultivar, has a high proportion of blooms in a limited spread of leaves.

- **Spread** 0.9–1.2m (3–4ft)
- **Planting depth** 30–45cm (12–18in)
- Hardy

Nymphaea 'Marliacea Carnea'

The light pink, day-blooming flowers are 11–12cm (4½–5in) across and have yellow stamens. Purplish young leaves mature to broadly ovate, dark green leaves, 17–20cm (7–8in) long. It is easily confused with *N.* 'Marliacea Rosea', which is a slightly deeper pink. It is particularly good for medium pools.

- **Planting depth** 30–45cm (12–18in)
- **Spread** 1.2–1.5m (4–5ft)
- Hardy

Nymphaea 'Marliacea Chromatella'

The free-flowering, canary yellow, day-blooming flowers are 15cm (6in) across, with broad, incurved petals and golden stamens. Coppery young leaves with purple streaks mature to purple-mottled, mid-green leaves, 15–20cm (6–8in) across. One of the best long-standing, reliable yellow waterlilies, this will perform satisfactorily in any pool.

- **Spread** 1.2–1.5m (4–5ft)
- **Planting depth** 30–45cm (12–18in)
- Hardy

Nymphaea 'Odorata Sulphurea Grandiflora' (syn. *N.* 'Sunrise')

The day-blooming, star-shaped flowers, with long, narrow, yellow petals, are 17–23cm (7–9in) across and have yellow stamens. Small areas of

Nymphaea 'Gonnère'

Nymphaea 'Lucida'

purple mottling are present on the young leaves, which mature to broadly ovate, plain green leaves, 27cm (11in) long and 25cm (10in) wide. Needing more warmth than most hardy waterlilies to develop its huge blooms, this cultivar is recommended for medium sized pools in warm temperate areas.

- **Spread** 1.2–1.5m (4–5ft)
- **Planting depth** 35–45cm (14–18in)
- **Hardy to slightly tender

Nymphaea 'Paul Hariot'

The changeable flowers are cup-shaped, 10cm (4in) across, slightly fragrant and held above the water, opening yellow, then changing with age to a darker, coppery-red, especially in the centre. The new leaves on young plants are speckled, then mature to oval, 15–18cm (6–7in) long, dark green with purple blotches. The flower size is deceptively large for a plant with such a limited spread, making it a good contender for tub cultivation.

- **Spread** 30–60cm (1–2ft)
- **Planting depth** 15–30cm (6–12in)
- Hardy

Nymphaea 'Pearl of the Pool'

The star-shaped, day-blooming, fragrant, pink flowers are 12–15cm (5–6in) across and have pinkish-orange stamens. Bronzed young leaves mature to round, green leaves, 25cm (10in) across. This flowers best when it is planted in a large planter so that it can form a cluster of roots.

- **Spread** 1.2–1.5m (4–5ft)
- **Planting depth** 30–45cm (12–18in)
- Hardy

Nymphaea 'Marliacea Chromatella'

NyNymphaea 'Pink Opal'

Cup-like, pink flowers, 8–10cm (3–4in) across and with a sweet fragrance, are held nearly 23cm (9in) above the water. Bronzy young leaves mature to round green leaves 23cm (9in) across. The pink flower buds are almost round. It is an excellent choice for tubs and bowls.

- **Spread** 30–60cm (1–2ft)
- **Planting depth** 15–23cm (6–9in)
- Hardy

Nymphaea 'Pink Sensation'

Nymphaea 'Pink Sensation'

The cup-shaped, day-blooming, pink flowers become star-shaped, 12–15cm (5–6in) across, with yellow inner stamens and pink outer ones. Purplish young leaves mature to round, green leaves, to 25cm (10in) across. This is one of the best pink cultivars that stay open late into the afternoon.

- **Spread** 1.2m (4ft)
- **Planting depth** 30–45cm (12–18in)
- Hardy

Nymphaea 'Pygmaea Helvola' (syn. *N. helvola*)

The slightly fragrant yellow flowers are cup-shaped, becoming star-shaped, 5–8cm (2–3in) across, and have yellow stamens. Oval, heavily mottled, purple-blotched leaves, 12cm (5in) long and 9cm (3½in) wide, with purple

Nymphaea 'Virginalis'

undersides. Superb for a barrel or sink.

- **Spread** 60cm (2ft)
- **Planting depth** 15–23cm (6–9in)
- Hardy

Nymphaea 'Pygmaea Rubra'

The tiny flowers, about 6cm (2½in) across, open dark pink or rose. The outer petals are white blushed with pink; with age they become a rich maroon red with orange stamens. The young leaves are bronzy, becoming almost round, 15–18cm (6–7in) across. It tends not to spread, making it particularly suitable for confined spaces. It flowers best in temperate pools in cooler water.

- **Spread** 30–60cm (1–2ft)
- **Planting depth** 15–23cm (6–9in)
- Hardy

Nymphaea 'Rose Arey'

The day-blooming, star-shaped, sweet-scented flowers are dark pink, 17–20cm (7–8in) across, with golden stamens that change to orange-pink towards the outside. Purple young leaves mature to round, plain green leaves, 23cm (9in) across. This does best in a large container or medium pool, where it can form a cluster of rhizomes that promote free flowering.

- **Planting depth** 38–60cm (15–24in)
- **Spread** 1.2–1.5 (4–5ft)
- Hardy

Nymphaea 'Saint Louis'

The day-blooming, star-shaped, fragrant flowers are lemon-yellow, 20–27cm (8–11in) across with golden-yellow stamens. Purple-blotched young leaves mature to broadly ovate, green leaves, sometimes with wavy edges, to 50cm (20in) long and 48cm (19in) wide. This, the first waterlily to be patented in the United States, is one of the best tropical lilies to try in

temperate areas in a conservatory with a minimum temperature of 10°C (50°F) and a medium-sized pool.

- **Planting depth** 38–60cm (15–24in)
- **Spread** 2.4–3m (8–10ft)
- Tender

Nymphaea tetragona (syn. *N.* 'Pygmaea Alba')

The dainty, star-like flowers rarely exceed 5cm (2in) across and have bright golden stamens. The leaves are small, only 5–8cm (2–3in) across, round and dark green with purple undersides. The smallest white cultivar, it is ideal for tubs, sinks and shallow pools.

- **Spread** 30–45cm (12–18in)
- **Planting depth** 15–30cm (6–12in)
- Hardy

Nymphaea 'Vésuve'

The fragrant, day-blooming flowers are star-shaped and glowing red, deepening in colour with age, 17cm (7in) across, with inward pointing petals and orange stamens. The almost circular green leaves are 23–25cm (9–10in) across. It has a long blooming season, in addition to opening early in the day and closing in late afternoon.

- **Spread** 1.2m (4ft)
- **Planting depth** 30–45cm (12–18in)
- Hardy

Nymphaea 'Virginalis'

The cup-shaped, day-blooming, fragrant, white flowers are 11–14cm (4½–5½in) across and have yellow stamens. Purple or bronze young leaves mature to round green leaves, 23cm (9in) across. A free-flowering, reliable cultivar, this is one of the best white hardy cultivars.

- **Spread** 0.9–1.2m (3–4ft)
- **Planting depth** 37–45cm (15–18in)
- Hardy

MARGINAL PLANTS

In addition to forming a decorative margin in shallow water, marginal plants help to produce clear water by removing excess nutrients from the pool through their roots. As long as they are grown in containers, the following are suitable for small to medium-sized pools. If you grow a selection of marginal plants, take care that late spring frosts do not damage some of the early-flowering plants such as *Lysichiton* spp.

If late frosts are forecast, protect flowers with horticultural fleece. If you have overwintered slightly frost-tender plants, such as lobelias and some forms of *Mimulus*, give the young emerging shoots a mulch, 5–8cm (2–3in) deep, of compost or organic humus-rich materials such as composted bark. The plants will shoot faster in the warm mulch, giving an opportunity of taking softwood cuttings if you want. If you have planted some of the larger moisture-lovers near the pool – *Gunnera manicata* or *Rheum* spp., for example – check they have a thick mulch over their crowns to prevent the margins of the leaves being browned with frost.

Although it is better to leave the planting of any new plants for in the pool until early summer, spring is a good time to plant young moisture-lovers at the pool side.

Acorus gramineus

Acorus calamus 'Variegatus'
Myrtle flag, sweet flag

A deciduous, perennial marginal with a spreading habit and distinctive, iris-like, erect mid-green leaves with a cream-striped variegation and occasional areas of wrinkling along the edges. The unusual flower resembles a small horn emerging laterally just below the tip of a leaf. It looks especially striking along the edges of a wildlife pool.

- **Height** 75cm (30in)
- **Spread** 60cm (2ft)
- **Water depth** to 23cm (9in)
- **Hardy**
- **Full sun**
- **Propagation** division of rhizomes

Acorus gramineus
Japanese rush

This is a superb plant for a small pool, and the grassy leaves make it suitable for the stream side as well. The pointed leaves are in two distinct ranks. There are several cultivars with variegated and coloured leaves.

- **Height** 20–30cm (8–12in)
- **Spread** 20–30cm (8–12in)
- **Water depth** to 8cm (3in)
- **Hardy**
- **Full sun**
- **Propagation** division of rhizomes

Alisma plantago-aquatica
Water plantain

A deciduous, perennial marginal, this has rosettes of oval, semi-upright leaves with long leaf stalks emerging above the water. The flower spike contains numerous small, pinkish-white flowers in summer. The seeds, which tend to set easily in the surrounding wet soil, are a valuable food supply for birds.

- **Height** 75cm (30in)
- **Spread** 45cm (18in)
- **Water depth** to 25cm (10in)
- **Hardy**
- **Full sun**
- **Propagation** seed or division

Butomus umbellatus
Flowering rush, water gladiolus

When it is planted in a container, this tall marginal can be grown successfully in a small pool, and it is particularly suitable for a wildlife pool. It is a most elegant plant, thriving in shallow water. The long, thin, dark green, triangular leaves are 1cm (½in) wide, and the flowerheads are full of individual reddish-white flowers held about 45–60cm (18–24in) above the leaves.

- **Height** 0.6–1.2m (2–4ft)
- **Spread** 45cm (18in)
- **Water depth** 8–13cm (3–5in)
- **Hardy**
- **Full sun**
- **Propagation** seed or division

Calla palustris
Bog arum

A deciduous or semi-evergreen perennial marginal, this has a long, conspicuous, creeping, surface root and round to heart-shaped, mid- to dark green, pointed leaves, which are

Carex elata 'Aurea'

glossy, firm and leathery. The flowers appear in spring, resemble small, flattened arum lilies and are followed by clusters of red or orange berries.

- **Height** 25cm (10in)
- **Spread** 30cm (12in)
- **Water depth** to 2in (5cm)
- Hardy
- Full sun
- **Propagation** seed or division of rhizomes

Caltha palustris
Marsh marigold, kingcup

One of the most popular marginals for the small pool, this has dark green, almost round leaves, which are heart-shaped at the base and have toothed margins. The familiar buttercup-like flowers are yellow and waxy, brightening early spring days.

- **Height** 15–30cm (6–12in)
- **Spread** 30cm (12in)
- **Water depth** to 8–10cm (3–4in)
- Hardy
- Full sun or partial shade
- **Propagation** seed or division

Caltha palustris var. *alba*
White marsh marigold

This varies from the species in producing white flowers slightly earlier in the year. It is also more compact and is ideal when the container is propped up inside a barrel or tub.

- **Height** 15–23cm (6–9in)
- **Spread** 23cm (9in)
- **Water depth** to 5–8cm (2–3in)
- Hardy
- Full sun or partial shade
- **Propagation** seed or division

Carex elata 'Aurea' (syn. *C. stricta* 'Aurea')
Bowles' golden sedge

This is a striking sedge for the margins of a pool. It has grass-like, narrow leaves and triangular flower stalks bearing flowers in brownish spikes in spring. The features that make it stand out as a suitable plant for the smaller pool are its vivid yellow foliage, which lasts well into summer, and its more compact habit than most sedges, although it needs to be restricted in a container in a small pool. Happy in shallow water, it does bet in moist soil that never dries out.

- **Height** 1m (3ft)
- **Spread** 45cm (18in)
- **Water depth** to 10–15cm (4–6in)
- Hardy
- Full sun
- **Propagation** seed or division

Cotula coronopifolia
Bachelor's buttons, brass buttons, golden buttons, water buttons

A bright little marginal for shallow water, this tends to be an annual or a short-lived perennial, regenerating vigorously in spring from the masses of seed produced the previous year. It has several creeping, succulent stems and fresh green, strongly scented, toothed leaves. In summer it is covered with masses of disc-shaped yellow flowers, each about 1cm (½in) across.

- **Height** 15–30cm (6–12in)
- **Spread** 30cm (12in)
- **Water depth** to 8–10cm (3–4in)
- Hardy
- Full sun
- **Propagation** seed or division

Darmera peltata (syn. *Peltiphyllum peltatum*)
Umbrella plant

This is an impressive plant for a small garden. The large, round leaves, from which it gets its common name, look beautiful reflected in the water. Pink flowers are produced before the leaves in spring on long, red-tinted stalks, reaching 30–60cm (1–2ft). Like the flowers, the leaves are held well above

Cotula coronopifolia

Darmera peltata

the soil on long stalks, often reaching 1m (3ft) high and 60cm (2ft) across. The round leaves are like heavily veined plates, with deeply lobed, coarsely toothed edges; they turn beautiful shades of pink and red in autumn. The roots form extensive, thick rhizomes, useful for binding wet or muddy soil.

- **Height** 1.2m (4ft)
- **Spread** 1m (3ft)
- **Water depth** 0–2.5cm (0–1in)
- **Hardy**
- **Full sun or partial shade**
- **Propagation** seed or division

Eriophorum angustifolium
Common cotton grass

This evergreen, perennial, marsh or marginal aquatic has a long rootstock. The short, angled stems bear grooved, grass-like, flat leaves. The conspicuous tassel-like flowers are white and downy. A common plant on acid moorland, it makes a good plant for a wildlife pool in boggy, shallow areas. It should be containerized in a small pool.

- **Height** 30–45cm (12–18in)
- **Spread** indefinite
- **Water depth** to 5cm (2in)
- **Hardy**
- **Full sun**
- **Propagation** division

Iris laevigata

Glyceria maxima var. *variegata*
Variegated water grass, sweet grass, manna grass

The striking leaves of this deciduous, perennial, spreading aquatic grass have cream, white and green stripes and are often tinged with pink at the base in spring and autumn. The flowers form greenish spikelets in summer. It is easy to grow and because it spreads rapidly must be kept in a container.

- **Height** 80cm (32in)
- **Spread** indefinite
- **Water depth** to 15cm (6in)
- **Hardy**
- **Full sun**
- **Propagation** seed or division

Houttuynia cordata

This deciduous, perennial marginal has clump-forming, spreading roots and erect, leafy red stems, bearing heart-shaped, pointed, highly aromatic, bluish-green, leathery leaves. In spring spikes of insignificant flowers are produced, and these are surrounded by white bracts. It benefits from a leafy mulch in winter because the stems are borderline in hardiness. It is very invasive, so keep it in a container.

- **Height** 15–60cm (6–24in)
- **Spread** indefinite
- **Water depth** to 2.5–5cm (1–2in)
- **Slightly tender**
- **Semi-shade**
- **Propagation** lift runners in spring

Houttuynia cordata 'Chameleon' (syn. *H. cordata* 'Tricolor')

This striking cultivar has variegated leaves in shades of crimson, cream and green, which are intensified in full sun.

- **Height** 15–60cm (6–24in)
- **Spread** indefinite
- **Water depth** to 2.5–5cm (1–2in)
- **Slightly tender**
- **Full sun**
- **Propagation** lift runners in spring

Houttuynia cordata 'Chameleon'

Iris laevigata

A fine iris for shallow water, this is deciduous, perennial marginal produces clumps of sword-shaped, smooth, soft green leaves with no midrib. The sparsely branched stem has from two to four broad-petalled, beardless blue flowers. It can be grown in a border if the soil never dries out.

- **Height** 60–90cm (2–3ft)
- **Spread** indefinite
- **Water depth** to 8–10cm (3–4in)
- **Hardy**
- **Sun or semi-shade**
- **Propagation** division of rhizomes

Iris laevigata 'Variegata'

Among the best variegated waterside plants, this has cream-striped leaves all summer. The flowers are paler blue than those of the species.

- **Height** 60–90cm (2–3ft)
- **Spread** indefinite
- **Water depth** to 8–10cm (3–4in)
- **Hardy**
- **Sun or semi-shade**
- **Propagation** division of rhizomes

Iris pseudacorus
Flag iris

A vigorous deciduous perennial marginal with thick roots, that grows in shallow water or moist soil. The broad, sword-like, ridged leaves are grey-green, and tall, branched flower stems bear as many as 10 beardless yellow flowers. The large, golden fall petals often have a dark patch in the centre. This must be grown in a container in a small pool. The variegated form is less vigorous and produces bright cream-striped yellow leaves in spring.

- **Height** 1.2m (4ft)
- **Spread** indefinite
- **Water depth** 0–30cm (0–12in)
- Hardy
- Sun or shade
- **Propagation** division of rhizomes

Iris versicolor
Blue flag, wild iris

This deciduous, perennial marginal has clump-forming, branched stems and sword-like, narrow, grey-green leaves. Each stem bears three to five violet-blue flowers with yellow patches at the petal bases, and the fall petals have a central white area and purple veins. It enjoys similar conditions to *I. laevigata*.

- **Height** 60cm (2ft)
- **Spread** indefinite
- **Water depth** to 5–8cm (2–3in)
- Hardy
- Semi-shade
- **Propagation** division of rhizomes

Juncus effusus f. spiralis (syn. Scirpus lacustris 'Spiralis')
Corkscrew rush

A curious little marginal plant for the shallow edges of small pools, where the dark green, corkscrew- and needle-like stems never fail to intrigue. If the stems revert to straight they should be removed straightaway.

- **Height** 30–45cm (12–18in)
- **Spread** 30–45cm (12–18in)
- **Water depth** 0–5cm (0–2in)
- Hardy
- Full sun
- **Propagation** division

Lysichiton americanus
Yellow skunk cabbage

A vigorous, deciduous, perennial marginal and moisture-loving aquatic, this has bright yellow, arum-like, unpleasantly scented flowers in early spring before the impressive, large, heavily veined, architectural green leaves, which can reach 1.2m (4ft). It needs a rich, deep soil and should be protected from cold winds and frost.

- **Height** 1m (3ft)
- **Spread** 1.2m (4ft)
- **Water depth** 2.5cm (1in)
- Hardy
- Full sun
- **Propagation** seed

Lysichiton camtschatcensis
White skunk cabbage

This is a good species of skunk cabbage for a small pool. Like *L. americanus*, it is a deciduous, perennial marginal or moisture-loving aquatic with a stout root and pure white, arum-like flowers in early spring. The paddle-like leaves, which are leathery, oblong to oval, heavily veined and bright green, are produced in loose rosettes. It is an excellent plant for streamside planting in rich, deep soil and slightly more compact than *L. americanus*.

- **Height** 75cm (30in)
- **Spread** 60–90cm (2–3ft)
- **Water depth** 2.5cm (1in)
- Hardy
- Full sun
- **Propagation** seed

Menyanthes trifoliata
Buckbean, bog bean, marsh trefoil

A deciduous, perennial, marginal, this has a thick, spongy, creeping rootstock, which often floats on the water. The shiny, clover-like, olive green leaves are made up of three leaflets with a long leaf stalk, which clasps the

rhizome with a broad sheath. Dainty, fringed, white to purplish flowers are produced from pink buds on a dense spike in spring. It needs a container to restrict it in a small pool.

- **Height** 23cm (9in)
- **Spread** indefinite
- **Water depth** 5cm (2in)
- Hardy
- Full sun
- **Propagation** division or cuttings

Myosotis scorpioides (syn. M. palustris)
Water forget-me-not

This deciduous, marginal perennial can be found growing wild in Europe in shallow mudbanks of still and slow-moving water in marshy meadows, ditches and pools. The creeping rhizome supports an angular stem, prostrate in the lower portions, becoming erect at the tips. It forms sprawling mounds of narrow, mid-green leaves, 10cm (4in) long, covered with short, rough hairs. In late spring to early summer it bears loose racemes of small forget-me-not, bright blue flowers, which have a central white, pink or yellow eye.

- **Height** 15–23cm (6–9in)
- **Spread** 30cm (12in)
- **Water depth** 0–2.5cm (0–1in)
- Hardy
- Full sun
- **Propagation** seed

Peltandra virginica (syn. P. undulata)
Green arrow arum

A deciduous, perennial marginal with narrowly arrow-shaped, firm, bright green leaves, 15–90cm (6–36in) long. The flowers resemble small arum lilies, narrow and strongly veined, 20cm (8in) tall, which turn yellow or white with waxy margins. They are followed by green berries in late summer.

- **Height** 90cm (3ft)
- **Spread** 60cm (2ft)
- **Water depth** 5–8cm (2–3in)
- **Hardy**
- **Full sun**
- **Propagation** division

Pontederia cordata
Pickerel weed

A robust, deciduous, perennial marginal, the pickerel weed is one of the most decorative blue-flowered aquatics. The thick, creeping root supports leaves that are dark green, tidy and erect with exquisite swirling. In late summer dense spikes of soft blue flowers are produced, appearing from a leaf bract at the top of the stem.

- **Height** 75cm (30in)
- **Spread** 45cm (18in)
- **Water depth** 13cm (5in)
- **Hardy**
- **Full sun**
- **Propagation** seed or division

Ranunculus flammula
Lesser spearwort

The aquatic genera of the large Ranunculaceae family tend to produce large, tall specimens that are suitable for the wildlife pool, but this species is suitable for the smaller pool. It creates a low-growing marginal, producing a succession of yellow flowers over summer. It has semi-prostrate, reddish stems and dark green, lance-shaped leaves, 1–2.5cm (⅜–1in) long. The bright yellow, cup-shaped flowers are 2cm (¾in) across and borne in clusters.

- **Height** 60cm (2ft)
- **Spread** 60cm (2ft)
- **Water depth** 8–10cm (3–4in)
- **Hardy**
- **Full sun**
- **Propagation** seed

Sagittaria latifolia
American arrowhead, duck potato, wapato

A deciduous, perennial marginal with spreading roots and soft green, arrow-shaped leaves, sometimes reaching 80cm (32in). Three-angled stems carry the white flowers in summer. Plants produce overwintering walnut-sized tubers at the ends of the roots, and these become detached in autumn. An excellent plant for the wildlife pool.

- **Height** 1.2m (4ft)
- **Spread** 60cm (2ft)
- **Full sun**
- **Hardy**
- **Propagation** seed

Sagittaria sagittifolia
Common arrowhead

This deciduous, perennial marginal has a short branching root and arrow-shaped leaves. In summer three-petalled white flowers appear in spikes on triangular flower stems. The upper male flowers on the spike have a violet centre. It prefers shallow water; flowering will be restricted in water deeper than 6in (15cm).

- **Height** 45cm (18in)
- **Spread** 30cm (12in)
- **Full sun**
- **Hardy**
- **Propagation** seed

Sagittaria sagittifolia 'Flore Pleno' (syn. *S. japonica*)
Japanese arrowhead

This is an excellent double form, bearing magnificent round, double-white flowers about 2.5cm (1in) across arranged around the flower stem.

- **Height** 45cm (18in)
- **Spread** 30cm (12in)
- **Full sun**
- **Hardy**
- **Propagation** division

Saururus cernuus
Lizard's tail, swamp lily, water dragon

A deciduous, perennial marginal with clump-forming, erect stems bearing heart-shaped, bright green leaves. The flowers are nodding spikes of waxy, fragrant, creamy flowers in summer. It is a distinctive specimen when planted slightly away from the margins.

- **Height** 23cm (9in)
- **Spread** 30cm (12in)
- **Water depth** 10–15cm (4–6in)
- **Hardy**
- **Full sun**
- **Propagation** division

Schoenoplectus lacustris subsp. *tabernaemontani* 'Zebrinus'
Bulrush

This perennial, spreading, marginal sedge has a strong root that creeps along the soil surface. Erect, leafless, dark green stems have horizontal cream banding. The flowers are white and brown terminal spikelets in summer. A dramatic plant, it needs a dark background to show off the unusual leaf banding. It must be containerized in a small pool.

- **Height** 1.5m (5ft)
- **Spread** indefinite
- **Water depth** 8–15cm (3–6in)
- **Hardy**
- **Full sun**
- **Propagation** division

Pontederia cordata

Typha minima

Zantedeschia aethiopica 'Green Goddess'

Scrophularia auriculata 'Variegata'
Water figwort

An evergreen, clump-forming perennial marginal with stiff, square stems carrying nettle-like leaves with creamy margins and a light green centre. The smaller leaves are almost entirely cream. Spikes of insignificant greenish-purple flowers are held above the foliage and are good for bees.

- **Height** 90cm (3ft)
- **Spread** 60cm (2ft)
- **Water depth** 8cm (3in)
- **Hardy**
- **Full sun**
- **Propagation** division

Typha minima
Reedmace

The only reedmace suitable for small pools, as most reedmaces swamp even medium and large pools easily. This species has narrow, needle-like leaves and attractive round, chocolate-brown flowerheads in late summer.

- **Height** 30–45cm (12–18in)
- **Spread** 45cm (18in)
- **Water depth** 0–10cm (0–4in)
- **Hardy**
- **Full sun**
- **Propagation** seed or division

Veronica beccabunga
Brooklime

A semi-evergreen, perennial, scrambling marginal with rather succulent, hollow, creeping stems, which root as they scramble over the wet soil. The short-stalked, fleshy leaves have blue flowers with white centres borne in their axils. An excellent scrambler for the edge and a mud bottom, but it is inclined to become straggly.

- **Height** 10cm (4in)
- **Spread** indefinite
- **Water depth** 8cm (3in)

- **Hardy**
- **Full sun**
- **Propagation** seed or division

Zantedeschia aethiopica 'Crowborough'
Arum lily, calla lily

A robust marginal, in summer this produces a succession of large, fragrant, white arum flowers, 8–25cm (3–10in) long, with a central yellow poker. The flower is surrounded by shiny, arrow-shaped, semi-erect, basal, dark green leaves. This cultivar is hardier than *Z. aethiopica* and will survive outdoors in winter provided it is covered with 30cm (1ft) of water; uncovered it needs a minimum temperature of 10°C (50°F). It is an excellent plant in a formal setting.

- **Height** 45–90cm (18–36in)
- **Spread** 35–45cm (14–18in)
- **Water depth** 30cm (12in)
- **Hardy**
- **Full sun**
- **Propagation** offsets in winter

Zantedeschia aethiopica 'Green Goddess'

This robust marginal produces a succession of green flowers, each with a large central green-splashed, white area, 8–25cm (3–10in) long, with a central yellow poker. The flower is surrounded by arrow-shaped, semi-erect, basal, dark green leaves. It is hardy when it is covered by 30cm (12in) of water. This is a good choice for a sunny corner of a formal pool.

- **Height** 45–90cm (18–36in)
- **Spread** 45–60cm (18–24in)
- **Water depth** 30cm (12in)
- **Hardy**
- **Full sun**
- **Propagation** offsets in winter

CHECKLIST OF SEASONAL CARE

The amount of seasonal care and maintenance you do will depend to a large extent on the contents of your water feature. Simple, self-contained features – wall fountains and cobble fountains, for example – will require little seasonal care, other than topping up the reservoirs in hot weather and cleaning the pump. Larger pools with plants and fish, on the other hand, will need more attention.

Season	Plants	Fish	General
Spring The pool water is at its clearest in spring, and as the days lengthen the fish become active and frog spawn can be seen. The fresh green leaves of the marginal plants will be starting into growth, and the early flowers, such as *Caltha palustris* (marsh marigold), will soon be in bloom. As life returns to the pool, now is the time to carry out the routine tasks that will prevent problems later in the year.	• Introduce new plants (page 136) • Divide waterlilies and deep-water aquatics every third or fourth year (page 138) • Remove the old leaves of marginal plants that are starting into growth, taking care not to damage new shoots (page 138) • Lift and divide marginal plants every two or three years (page 138) • If late frosts are forecast, protect vulnerable plants with horticultural fleece (page 149) • Prune plants grown for their winter stems hard back (page 135) • Discourage algal growth in the shallower regions of the pool when there are few waterlily leaves to shade the water and the oxygenators have not started into growth by scattering *Lemna* spp. (duckweed) on the surface to provide shade (page 134)	• Feed only if the water temperature is above 10°C (50°F) and use wheatgerm pellets until the water temperature is a degree or two higher, when protein-rich food should be given (page 130) • Protect vulnerable pools from attacks from herons (page 131) • Examine fish for signs of pests and disease (page 131)	• Remove electric pool heaters • Check pumps that were left in the water over winter in case the strainer has become clogged with decaying leaves or algae • Scrub off algae from any paving surfaces around the pool (page 109)
Summer Summer is the busiest time in the pool year, and the beauty of waterlily flowers dominates the pool. Unfortunately, it is also the time of year when algae and pests can get a hold quickly, and in a small pool their effect is more noticeable and disfiguring.	• This is a good time to lift the planting crates and divide the marginals (page 138) • Remove yellow and brown waterlily leaves so that they do not sink to the bottom and rot (page 145) • Cut back oxygenators, which can easily reach the surface of a shallow pool and spread too extensively under water, and use the young shoots as softwood cuttings if more stock is required (page 138) • Feed waterlilies with slow-release fertilizer sachets (page 138) • Collect seed to increase stocks of plants that are difficult to divide (page 137) • Introduce tender or exotic floating plants for extra interest (page 142)	• Fish will be eating voraciously now; supplement their diet with fresh food, which should be available now (page 130) • Remove blanketweed before it becomes so thick that it traps small fish • Keep fountains or waterfalls running on hot summer nights to supplement depleted oxygen supplies or spray the surface vigorously with a narrow-jet hosepipe to create enough turbulence for the water to absorb extra oxygen (page 130)	• Check the strainer on the pump; clogging with blanketweed or debris will soon affect the performance • Keep topping up the water level (page 37)
Autumn As the days shorten and the temperature falls, life in and around the pool slows down and prepares for winter.	• Protect tender moisture-loving plants with leaves (page 135) • Remove tender floating plants, such as *Eichhornia crassipes* (water hyacinth) or *Pistia stratiotes* (water lettuce), to overwinter in frost-free conditions (page 135) • Cut back the oxygenators hard as these will die back and rot in the water in winter (page 138) • For neatness, cut back the old brown stems of marginals in a formal pool but leave them in place in wildlife or informal pools to provide winter cover for small creatures (page 129)	• Gradually reduce the amount of food offered and use wheatgerm pellets as the water cools down (page 130) • Stop feeding altogether when the temperature drops to 10°C (50°F) (page 130)	• Prevent falling leaves from landing on the water with netting (page 18) • Pumps that are not likely to be used during the winter months can be removed over winter • In areas that have mild winters, biological filters should be kept running as algae can still grow in the winter (page 37)
Winter Even in winter there can be mild, sunny days where the low angle of light and hoar frost can add a special beauty to moving water.	• Take pygmy and tender waterlilies indoors if prolonged severe weather is likely (page 145)	• Leave fish undisturbed in the warmer water on the pool bottom • Avoid disturbing the layer of warmer water by elevating any pump that is working so that it circulates the colder surface water only	• Prevent an unbroken layer of ice forming on the surface of the pool with an electric pool heater or a pan of hot water

INDEX

Page numbers in *italics* refer to the illustrations

ACKNOWLEDGEMENTS

Heather Angel 24 Top, 24 Bottom, 126, 129, 130 Centre, 130 Bottom.

Ardea/D. Avon 128 Top, /Brian Bevan 128 Bottom.

Bradshaws Direct Ltd (tel:01904 691169 www.bradshawsdirect.co.uk) 36 Top, 36 Centre, 36 Bottom.

Adrian Bloom Horticultural Library/Richard Bloom 150 Bottom Right.

Mark Bolton 7, 93, 96, /Design: Bob Purnell 22, 38, /Garden Planners 4.

Eric Crichton/Design: C. Costin, Hampton Court 1997 108 Top, /Design: Marney Hall & Paul Dyer, Chelsea Show 1998 90, /Design: Merrist Wood College, Chelsea Show 1994 117 Top, /Private Garden 40 Top, /Design: Geoff Whiten, Chelsea Show 1995 Yardley/Express Garden 52.

Emap Gardening Picture Library 54, 110 Top, 115, 118, 121.

Elizabeth Whiting Associates (www.elizabethwhiting.com) 109, /Karl Dietrich-Buhler 119, /Jerry Harpur 18, 98.

Frank Lane Picture Agency/Alwyn J Roberts 140.

Garden Picture Library/Eric Crichton 153, /Christopher Fairweather 137, 143 Bottom,/Vaughan Fleming 142 Top, 151 Top Right, /John Glover 28, 145, /John Glover/Design: Sarah Raven, Chelsea Flower Show 1998 139, /Michael Howes 136,/Jacqui Hurst/Design:

Ann Frith 10, 13, /Marie O'Hara 132, 154 Top Left, /Jerry Pavia 141 Bottom, 149, /Howard Rice 31 Bottom Left, 144 Top Left, 147 Top Centre, 150 Bottom Centre, /Gary Rogers 110 Bottom, /Alec Scaresbrook 138 Top, 138 Bottom, /Ron Sutherland 17, 19, 62, /Ron Sutherland/Design: Anthony Paul 116, /Ron Sutherland/Design: Paul Fleming 42, /Juliette Wade 143 Top Right.

John Glover 14 Top Centre, 142 Bottom, 148 Top Left, /Design: David Anderson, Hampton Court 1998 112 Right, /Design: Crockett/Summers 14 Top Right, /Design: Chris Jacobson 40 Bottom, /Design: Dowle/Gordon 47, /Fairfield, Surrey 77, /Hampton Court 1992 88, /Ladywood, Harts 78, /Design: Hiroshi Nanamori 64-65 Centre, /Design: OUDLF/Maynard 8 Top, /Private Garden, Shropshire 25, /Design: Robin Templar Williams 21.

Harpur Garden Library/Design: Simon Fraser/Sarah Robinson, London 82, /Design: Gunilla Pickard, Essex 74, /Design: Roger Platts, RHS Chelsea Show 8 Bottom, /RHS Chelsea Garden Societies 1999 106 Top Right, /C & D Rothman, Philadelphia, USA 16 Top, /Design: Mark Rumary, Suffolk 107, /Jacqui Small 16 Bottom, /Franchesca

Watson, Cape Town, RSA 27 Bottom, /Design: Robin Williams, London 29.

Hozelock Cyprio 34 Top.

Hugh Palmer/Design: Ian Stubbs 113.

Andrew Lawson 6, 60, 69, 73, 112 Left, 144 Bottom, 147 Top Right, 148 Bottom, 151 Bottom Left, 154 Bottom Left, /Design: Paul Bangay 2, 122, /Design: Andrew Card 117 Bottom, /Moss Green, New Zealand 1, /Hampton Court Flower Show 2000 104, 106 Bottom Left, /RHS Chelsea 1997 9.

Lotus Water Gardens (tel: 0208 686 2231 www.lotuswatergardens.com) 26 Top, 26 Centre, 26 Bottom, 27 Top, 32 Top Left, 32 Top Right, 32 Bottom.

Marianne Majerus/Design: Robert Clark 50, /Coworth Garden Design & Construction 56, /Design: Andrew Harman & Jon Norton 37, /Design: Rosemary Lindsay 58.

S & O Mathews 14 Bottom, 147 Bottom Right, 150 Top Left.

Natural Image/Bob Gibbons 141 Top.

Clive Nichols Photography/The Anchorage, Kent 68, /Brinsby College, Chelsea 2000 85, /Brook Cottage, Oxon 135, /Chelsea 1994 48, /Chelsea 1995 35, /Design: Olivia Clarke 44, /Garden & Security Lighting, Hampton Court 1997 124, /Lighting: Garden & Security Lighting/Design:

Natural & Oriental Water Gardens 123, /Little Coopers, Hampshire 66, 81, 100, /Design: Clare Mathews 41, /The Nichols Gdn, Reading, fountain design: Fiona Barrett/Lighting: Garden & Security Lighting 125, /Wollerton Old Hall, Shropshire 103.

Oase UK Ltd (tel: 01264 333225) 34 Top Centre, 34 Bottom, 34 Bottom Centre.

Photos Horticultural 146.

Red Cover/Hugh Palmer 84, /Hugh Palmer/Design: Robert Simpson 12.

Derek St Romaine 30, 131, /Design: Mr & Mrs Lusby, Whitehouse Farm Cottage 31 Bottom Right, /RHS Hampton Court 1997, Pet Friendly Garden, /Design: Clare Palgrave 86, /Mrs Maureen Thompson, Sun House, Long Melford, Suffolk 33.

Nicola Stocken Tomkins/Design: Paul Dyer 71, /Design: Elizabeth Gage 31 Top, /Design: Robin Templar Williams 15.

Sunniva Harte/Groombridge Gdns, Kent 108 Bottom.

Jo Whitworth/Barleywood/ Design: Alan Titchmarsh 120, /Exbury Gardens, Hants 95, /RHS Gardens, Wisley 99.

Rob Whitworth RHS Hampton Court Palace Flower Show /Design: Simon Charter 134